Hollywood Parables

JOHN BOARDMAN

Cover design by Erika Duran
Insta @erikartgalerij
https://easduran.myportfolio.com/portfolio

Chapter illustrations by Liz Bruce
Insta @lizb001

ISBN: 9798405541969

To Alison

CONTENTS

ACKNOWLEDGMENTS

My thanks go first to Steve Thomson, Mark Elder and Andy Browning for supporting the Reel Deal initiative at St. Peter's Baptist Church whence this book emerged. These pastors had the foresight and political savvy to facilitate the hijacking of a monthly Sunday evening service to allow the exploration of God's divine character through the medium of popular film. May God forgive you!

My oldest and dearest friend Peter Gold, whose literary skills far exceed mine, read through all of the draft chapters as they gradually emerged through rewrite, edit and trashing, and provided invaluable feedback. This allowed something resembling an intelligible, perhaps even enjoyable read to evolve.

Whatever else this exchange achieved, it at least persuaded Peter to cease being an atheist and turn to agnosticism. Having finally left the station of unbelief Peter, may God accompany you on your journey of doubt that ends with Him.

Many gifted friends devoted their time and talents to the Reel Deal program, far too many to name them all. I must of necessity single out Rich Tarbox, Paul Kippax, Tim Breed, Rob Marshall and Tim Dean. Thank you for inspiring me to scale new heights.

My sincere thanks go to Liz Bruce for her charcoal drawings of the unforgettable Melvin Udall, Del & Neal, Spartacus, George Bailey and Andy Dufresne. I hope that the literary portrayal of these characters honours your amazing artistry.

My grateful thanks go to a host of anonymous volunteers who reviewed the draft MS and provided useful marketing material to promote the book.

Thank you IMDB.com - the premier resource for film lovers. The dialogue reproduced in this work is taken from your relevant pages. It has been suitably edited to reduce offensive language for those of a sensitive disposition.

For the authentic version of what the characters actually say, there are always the original films. I encourage you to watch them, and to do so with God by your side. If you do you will hear the deeper meanings that convey His truth and love to you.

Finally, the greatest debt I owe is to my darling wife, Alison. She daily shows me so much mercy and grace and exhibits life-giving joy continually. When I falter, she urges me on; when I doubt, she points the way; and, when I despair, she reminds me what is important.

She is my Bedford Falls. She makes me want to live again.

HOLLYWOOD PARABLES

1 AS GOOD AS IT GETS

THE EXPERT LOVER

Melvin knows all there is to know about love. His 61 best-selling novels on romantic fiction are testimony to this knowledge. This love has made Melvin a very rich man and his riches enable him to manifest this love in many ways. Let me offer you a few illustrations of Melvin's love.

Firstly, he cares for the environment. A dog that wanders off from their owner to urinate in the hallway is clearly harmful to the environment, especially the bit that adjoins Melvin's luxury apartment. So, with characteristic love Melvin teaches one such offender a lesson about cleanliness he won't forget in a hurry. The stray sprayer is snatched by gloved hands and dispatched down the chute to rendezvous with the garbage truck in the basement where he can help clean up the environment by eating diaper dirt. Melvin knows much about love.

Secondly, Melvin cares for his neighbour, enough to educate the ignoramus on the critical value of his use of home as office. Melvin is about to complete work on his

62nd book in the solitude of his apartment. It will be yet another epic on the meaning of love. His is an uninterruptable act of creation. Unfortunately, Simon, the gay neighbour, is blissfully unaware of this fact. Simon had lost Verdell but a diligent janitor has retrieved the miserable mutt from the garbage truck in the basement. He offers a tentative explanation of how Verdell could possibly have got there – *"Maybe some kind neighbour shoved him down the garbage chute?"* Simon wonders if that *kind neighbour* is Melvin.

The incessant banging on Melvin's apartment door is a regrettable distraction from creative artistry but in disguise it presents a great opportunity for Melvin to show love to his neighbour by bringing the artist painter into the picture. Here's how the conversation between Simon and Melvin goes …

"I found Verdell Mr Udall"

"Well that's a load off!"

"Did you do something to him?"

"Do you realise that I work at home?"

"Well er huh no"

"Do you like to be interrupted when you're nancying around in your little garden?"

"Well er huh no er actually. I'll turn the ringer off my phone and er …"

"Well I work all the time, so never never interrupt me ok? Not if there's a fire, not even if you hear the sound of a thud from my home and one week later there's a smell coming from there that can only be a decaying human body and you have to hold a hanky to your face because the stench is so thick that you think you're going to faint. Even then, don't come knocking. Or, if it's election night, and you're excited and you want to celebrate because somebody that you date has been elected the first queer president of the United States and he's going to have you down to Camp David, and you want someone to share the moment with. Even then, don't knock. Not on this door. Not for ANY reason. Do you get me, sweetheart?"

How could Simon not get it? What could be clearer? Thanks Melvin. Your use of '*sweetheart*' says it all. Melvin knows a lot about love.

Another great example of Melvin's love for people is his obsessive care for Carol. She is the one and only waitress he wants as his server when eating at his favourite diner. Such is Melvin's devotion to Carol that he will not seek, nor shall he accept, any surrogate bringing him his breakfast. This incidentally is a point of view with which all the other servers happily concur.

On one occasion Carol is absent from her post, which enrages Melvin who is slightly obsessive and may have OCD. The café owner's patience with Melvin is completely exhausted so he finally evicts the bewildered writer but not before he is mercifully able to ascertain Carol's home address.

Melvin now takes on a mission to establish the cause of Carol's absence and to do all he can to rectify the situation. Thanks to his vast resources and extensive influence his powers to remedy any situation are considerable.

It transpires that Carol is unable to be at the diner not because she is sick but because her son is sick. Melvin recalls a previous conversation with Carol …

"Okay, so what's with the plastic utensils? Why not try ours? Afraid it isn't clean? Just give yourself a little pep talk. 'Must try other people's clean silverware as part of the fun of dining out.'"

"What's wrong with your son anyway?"

"He's gotta fight to breathe. His asthma can just shoot off the charts -- he's allergic to dust and this is New York and his immune system bails on him when there's trouble so an ear infection... Is this bothering you?"

"No"

"An ear infection can send us to the emergency room -- maybe five, six times a month where I get whatever nine-year-old they just made a doctor. Nice chatting with you."

"His name"

"Spencer"

"Okay"

"Spence".

Notice how Melvin deftly overlooks Carol's sarcasm about Melvin's preferred use of his own plastic utensils, focussing instead, with laser-like concern, on her son's health. And notice also how Melvin persists in his investigations by wanting to know the boy's name. Maybe Melvin is a praying person and needs to get specific in his intercessions? Melvin cares.

Melvin can help Spence get better, help Carol get back to work, make her and her family's life better and ultimately do some good for himself. No harm in that. Melvin knows a great deal about love.

So, Melvin makes a plan and executes it with breath-taking skill. He speaks to his editor who is married to a top doctor who then visits Carol and examines Spencer closely. Dr. Bettes is confident that the boy is going to feel much better in hardly anytime at all. The expenses, which are considerable, will all be billed to Melvin. Melvin knows a lot about love.

Carol is of course obligated, and she obsesses that Melvin has an ulterior motive, one that horrifies her. She cannot sleep. She must be put at ease. Melvin must be made aware. So, Carol visits Melvin even though it is a midnight run across the East River. She accepts Melvin's care but not at any price.

Here's how that conversation goes ….

"Carol, the waitress?"

"Yes. The doctors had your billing address. I'm sorry about the hour"

"I was working. Can't you just drop me a thank you note"

"That's not why I'm here…. though you have no idea what it's like to have a real conversation with a doctor about Spencer…"

"Note. Put it in a note"

"Why did you do this for me?"

"To get you back to work so you can wait on me".

"But you do have some idea how strange that sounds??? I'm worried that you did this because ... "

There's a pregnant pause ... broken by Melvin.

"You waiting for me to say something? What sort of thing do you want? Look, I'll be at the restaurant tomorrow."

"I don't think I can wait until tomorrow, this needs clearing up."

"What needs clearing up?"

"I'm not going to sleep with you. I will never, ever sleep with you. Never. Not ever".

"I'm sorry. We don't open for the no-sex oaths until 9 a.m."

"I'm not kidding".

"Okay. Anything else?"

"No"

"So you'll be at work tomorrow?"

"Yes"

Notice how Melvin lovingly deflects Carol's careless aspersion that Melvin has acted egregiously by rescuing Spence in exchange for prospective sexual favours – '*We don't open for the no-sex oaths until 9 a.m.*'!

Still, Carol has her suspicions. She can hardly believe that this man, who undoubtedly has acted extraordinarily sacrificially, has done so simply in order that she can bring him breakfast. What does Melvin see in her that makes her so special? Good question. Remember, Melvin knows a lot about love.

There's one final example of Melvin's love that is well worth sharing, and that concerns healing. This is not the kind that Dr. Bettes was able to bring to Carol's son Spencer. This is an emotional healing that is needed when

5

people are deeply wounded psychologically, through some kind of trauma perhaps in which they are innocent victims.

This account involves a trip to Baltimore but the background to this trip is important to understand.

Simon had been viciously attacked while working at home. He was robbed, badly beaten and needed hospitalisation. His one chance of recovery was to beg his parents for money. This was no easy task because Simon's father could never come to terms with homosexuality. One time he found Simon painting his mother in the nude and he was horrified. He forced the young Simon to leave home giving him a 'thick wad of sweaty money' and telling him never to return.

Now it should be said that Melvin also disapproves of homosexuality and is intensely wary of 'queers' - as he might refer to them. Queers choose to go their own way and that can make them exceedingly self-centred. Melvin knows this is not in their best interests so a firm rebuke, lovingly delivered is appropriate medicine, or so Melvin reasons. (This explains Melvin's uncompromising speech to Simon regarding the lost and found Verdell).

However, Melvin became the object of loving insistence when Frank, the agent who exhibits Simon's work, was suitably persuasive when Simon was hospitalised. Frank was equally impressive in getting Melvin to 'volunteer' to drive Simon to Baltimore. Perhaps Melvin thought that Simon would repent, turn away from the gay life, and be restored to his father much like the prodigal son was? However, Melvin needed an insurance policy in case Simon made overtures to him. Carol was that safeguard. It would be a way of her showing her thankfulness for the extraordinary kindness Melvin had shown her.

Things did not go that well. Simon met a wall of silence from his parents and sank deeper into depression. Carol wanted to celebrate her son's recovery, so Melvin was her date. She told Melvin, 'If you ask me I'll say yes' so Melvin suggested that 'maybe you could sleep with Simon'.

Now of course this statement can be easily misinterpreted. Undoubtedly, in his infinite wisdom Melvin would see his suggestion as part of Simon's recovery from being a queer and so being restored to his parents. Carol saw it differently. Melvin was now assuming the role of her pimp assigning Carol as he saw fit to various needy cases.

Anyway, things got out of hand and Melvin had cause to reflect on the fact that love might actually be a more complex matter then he had come to understand it, and that perhaps he did not know as much about the subject as his library of published work superficially indicated.

Here, I think, is how Melvin saw it. Simon had an ailment – he loved men not women. If he could be persuaded, then he could be healed of this ailment, and sleeping with Carol was as good a first step as any. Melvin knew her virtues or so he thought.

She, on the other hand, wasn't in a relationship. She was unmarried and found dating hard caring primarily for her beloved son. She lived at home with her mom whose husband was also not around. Carol was being denied what any young attractive woman her age should be able to count on – plenty of healthy heterosexual activity. Carol had made clear this was not going to be with Melvin. So Melvin put two and two together – but unfortunately came up with five. What went wrong with the calculation?

I guess people are no more understood in terms of numbers than love is understood from the pages of romantic fiction.

Now Melvin faced an existential crisis. What did his voluminous library of published novels amount to? Were all those dramatic narratives simply nonsense? Was the love that he wrote about real or fictitious? Was his love for others real or a figment of his imagination? Did he love himself, not in a selfish narcissistic sense, but healthily and in a way that brought others health?

For answers to these and related questions we need to look at a few more incidents in the life of Melvin that may shed some light.

THE SICK PUPPY

Homophobia is not the only fear that Melvin has. To his list of pet hates must be added - women, blacks, Jews and dogs. Let's go over this list.

It's quite possible that Melvin's intentions towards Verdell were not entirely virtuous. As he picked him up with gloved hands he declared '*You've peed your last*'. As he tossed him down the garbage chute he announced '*This is New York. If you can make it here, you can make it anywhere*'. And with that, the furry mutt felt the full force of gravity.

Melvin once complained to Carol '*I got Jews at my table*'. Then to hasten their departure from his table he somewhat rudely declared '*your appetites are not as big as your noses huh?*' That was enough for them. They left.

Melvin was intensely suspicious of blacks and maybe feared them as a race that would finally exact their revenge on the whites who had bound them in slavery for two centuries in the land of the free.

Finally, although Melvin wrote women so well, when asked by an adoring female fan how he managed to do this he extinguished her adulation with this fire hose, '*I think of a man and I take away reason and accountability*'.

Now these incidents taken individually can conceivably be explained as rational fears grounded in truth and exercised with measured love. Hmmm! However, taken as a whole, they cannot be so easily dismissed.

As a totality they may point to a compulsive disorder that has metastasized into collection of deep-rooted fears, such as xenophobia, homophobia, and germaphobia, and irrational ingrained hatreds like misogyny and racism. Add narcissism for bad measure. This represents a dreadfully destructive combination.

We may need to concede that Melvin may not be the greatest lover of mankind that we first imagined. His knowledge of love may be an invention of a creative mind, which does not actually find its way into empathetic daily relations and sincere transactions.

Melvin, put simply, may not be the person we initially cracked him up to be. There may be something wrong with Melvin and what's more there are good reasons to believe that Melvin realises this for himself. Here are three instances.

Firstly, when Melvin was acting as Simon's dog sitter, he developed a regular routine of walking the dog with him to his diner and back to his apartment. Verdell would be tied to a lamppost outside the restaurant, which Melvin could see from his table. Thus, Melvin could eat his food as normal, keep the dog outside, which is to be expected, yet keep an eye on the animal to ensure his safety.

One of Melvin's curious perambulatory habits was to avoid the cracks in the sidewalk. Who knows why? It is part of his OCD. After days of trailing alongside his new minder Verdell picked up this habit and we find this diminutive Brussels Griffin skipping over the cracks in the sidewalk. It's utterly hilarious. Melvin notices this canine curiosity and is emotionally stirred at the sight. It is both amusing and sobering. He picks up Verdell and lifts him on high above his head. This time there's no threat of a garbage chute, those days are long gone. He says to Verdell 'Now don't you be like me'.

It is the most loving of rebukes. It is a warning to the dog and to us. Melvin knows his behaviour is aberrant. He wished he could change. He has seen a therapist and been given medication. He hates pills. He no longer sees his therapist. He continues with his OCD but wishes he could be rid of it. He doesn't want the dog mimicking strange behaviour. He is effectively saying to himself 'my behaviour needs to change. He doesn't know how.

Melvin cares for Verdell and maybe that's a start.

Here is a second hopeful sign. The one true love of Melvin's life is Carol, but he has a hard time realising that for himself. It's not until he makes himself vulnerable to Simon that he is made aware that Carol is the one that he wants, and therefore he needs to come clean with her. There is one episode where Melvin lets Carol know what he truly thinks of her. It's a beautiful moment worth reflecting on because it also lets us know that Melvin knows he has a problem.

During the Baltimore trip Carol has made Melvin take her on a date. They are at a fancy restaurant which borders onto the Patapsco River that flows into the great Atlantic Ocean. Hard shell crab dinners are the speciality. Dancing is a possibility. A cocktail or two relaxes Carol but it is Melvin that has the floor. He seeks to pay Carol a compliment. This is their conversation ...

"I've got a really great compliment for you, and it's true".

"I'm so afraid you're about to say something awful".

"Don't be pessimistic; it's not your style. Okay, here I go: Clearly, a mistake. I've got this, what - ailment? My doctor, a shrink that I used to go to all the time, he says that in fifty or sixty per cent of the cases, a pill really helps. I hate pills, very dangerous thing, pills. Hate. I'm using the word hate here, about pills. Hate. My compliment is, that night when you came over and told me that you would never... all right, well, you were there, you know what you said. Well, my compliment to you is, the next morning, I started taking the pills"

"I don't quite get how that's a compliment for me".

"You make me want to be a better man"

"That's maybe the best compliment of my life"

Think about that line ...

"You make me want to be a better man"

What does it say? If we break it down it says an immense amount. Here's my takeaway …

" … there's something wrong with me, and I know there is. There's nothing I can do about it and it won't get any better if I do nothing. I'm trapped but I want to escape. My doc is offering me an escape tunnel. This tunnel is built of pills. I hate pills. I'm using the word hate to describe pills. This tunnel is so disagreeable that I don't want to enter it, but it's my only chance.

When I think of you, I think maybe I could take the pills – even though I hate the pills. But if I take the pills, if I enter this tunnel made of pills, then maybe I will find a way out of my life that I hate to discover my true identity and find you.

When I think of you, I can take the pills, face the tunnel, find the exit, escape this ailment stricken life and be with you. You make me want to be a better man."

I think that's what this line is saying. Melvin knows everything there is to know about love. Yet Melvin knows nothing. But he knows he knows nothing, in spite of his 62 romantic novels. He knows what he knows and he knows that he is not a well man but he wants to be a better man and he believes that Carol might be the way.

Melvin's love for Carol is the next step in his redemption.

There's one final clue that tells us, if we're listening, that Melvin is not the love expert that he and we thought he was when we kicked off this parable. It's a conversation that emerges when our three main characters are on their way to Baltimore. They are in Frank's car, which is now being driven by Carol. Melvin takes a back seat – appropriately. Melvin has introduced the other two to each other with the immortal line: *"Carol the waitress – Simon the fag"*

These monikers tell us a lot about Melvin. He has his people conveniently labelled, happily circumscribed like the fictional characters he paints in his works of romantic fiction.

But real people are the product of finer brush strokes and a palette of infinite colours. People are not denoted by one-word conveniences.

Having introduced them their relationship is beyond Melvin's control. By drawing each of them into his life he has created without realising it a mighty fusion that releases great energy into the world, a force that might well be for good, a dynamic that can deliver radical change even in Melvin's life which is not as great as we might first think or under his control as his OCD might wish.

So, let's join our three 'heroes' in Frank's car. Remember Carol is driving and wants to know more about Simon. Melvin is in the back seat annoyed that things are not going to his plan. He is listening passively. Carol speaks first....

"I'm sure, Simon, they did something really "off" in order for you to feel this way. But when it comes to your parents or your kids, something will always be "off" unless you set it straight. And maybe this thing happened to you so you have a chance to do that."

Melvin tries to interrupt.

"Nonsense! And you want to know why?"

Carol wants to put this to a vote!

"Anybody here who's interested in what Melvin has to say, raise their hands."

Melvin doesn't get to interrupt anymore!

"Do you want to know what happened with my parents?"

"Yes... no, wait. I'm gonna pull over and give you my full attention. Now go ahead."

"When I was a kid, I always painted, and my mother always encouraged it. She was sort of fabulous about it, actually. And she used to... I was too young to think that there was anything wrong with it, and she was very natural, so she used to... pose nude for me. I always thought - or I assumed - my father knew about it. One day he found us and started screaming. I was trying to defend my mother and make peace in the lamest way. I said "she's not naked, it's art. And he started hitting me and... he beat me unconscious. He taught me a lesson he thought I'd never forget. I mean, he knew what I was even before I did. And the morning I left for college, he walked into my room and held out his hand, and it was filled with money. A big, sweaty wad of money. And he said, "I don't want you to ever come back." I grabbed him and hugged him... and he turned around and walked out. I haven't seen him or talked to him since."

Carol kisses Simon on the cheek. Melvin notices. It's not his cheek. He wants a kiss on his cheek. Why is his cheek not being kissed? Carol speaks ...

"We all have these terrible stories to get over, and you..."

From the back seat ...

"It's not true. Some of us have great stories, pretty stories that take place at lakes with boats and friends and noodle salad. Just no one in this car. But a lot of people, that's their story. Good times, noodle salad. What makes it so hard is not that you had it bad, but that you're ticked off that so many others had it good."

"No I don't think so"

"No, not it at all really"

Melvin is in a minority of one. Why is this? Or is there something in common between the three of them that we're missing, something that would explain the nature of all their injuries? If we look carefully at what gets said what do we infer? The one thing, the one key phrase that lives in this fabulous dialogue is this one ... "Just no one in this car!"

What Melvin is saying, I think, is that all three of them have missed out on a great childhood that has robbed them of their peace, has left them deeply wounded on the inside, has planted considerable doubt in their minds that reflects on lack of self-esteem and heightened insecurity. What is it?

THE FAULT LINES

I conclude that what our three characters in this story share is faulty parenting. We know that to be the case for Simon. I necessarily surmise this for Carol and Melvin but with defensible logic.

We don't find Carol's dad in the picture, just her mom. Maybe he was a great dad and he passed away. Maybe. Or maybe he was a bad husband and poor father and left. That leaves scars.

Spencer's dad is also missing. Maybe he too died, or maybe he left. That leaves more scars, more room for doubt and a painful reminder of an unhappy childhood.

Carol the waitress appears utterly serene. She is efficient, polite, warm-hearted, big-hearted. I bet she gets great tips. But underneath all of this delightful serenity there lies a fragile human being. We see this in a heart to heart with her mom and when Carol is at her wits end. I think Carol missed her dad.

We just don't know about Melvin, but something caused his OCD. Maybe it is a genetic disorder, or maybe a consequence of severe discipline in the family home that insisted on order with little reward for doing good and maximal punishment for making errors. We just don't know. But we do know Melvin knew about…

"pretty stories that take place at lakes with boats and friends and noodle salad… a lot of people, that's their story. Good times, noodle salad. Just no one in this car. What makes it so hard is not that you had it bad, but that you're that ticked off that so many others had it good"

Just no one in this car! That includes Melvin. He knew about pretty stories, lakes and boats and friends. He knew about good times and noodle salad, but maybe he did not know it personally. Maybe he read it in a book. Maybe love happened in books but no one ever kissed you on the cheek.

But now at least Melvin has BOTH Carol and Simon. He might make it out of the tunnel with their combined help.

THE PICTURE'S PARABLE

The story of Melvin, Carol and Simon is of course the story of the 1997 film *As good as it gets* starring Jack Nicholson, Helen Hunt and Greg Kinnear.

Mr Nicholson and Miss Hunt won Oscars for Best Actor and Best Actress – Mr Kinnear was nominated.

It is a great movie and can be truly regarded as a classic. In fact, as far as greatness is concerned, this film could properly be said to be as good as it gets!

I love to watch it regardless of how many times I've already seen it. When I do, I am enjoying the company of a friend with all its familiarity of dialogue, dramatic movement, facial expression and pregnant silences. But in seeing it again I never fail to find something new about it; another layer of meaning, another nuance revealed, one more subtle point that I may have missed.

As much as I already know this old and dear friend, I still discover something new. That abiding appreciation is testimony to the deeper meanings of the film regardless of whether these were intended by the film's makers, whether it is simply serendipitous, or whether there was some invisible hand painting a secret picture for those with eyes to see and ears to hear.

I am obliged, in including this film in my short list of Hollywood Parables to say what I believe these deeper meanings to be. In a nutshell *As good as it gets* provides us with a message that lets us know two vitally important truths.

First, that ***the things we cannot control are the very things that can free us from the compulsion to control.***
Secondly, ***the way to love others is to learn to love***

ourselves healthily.

This film whilst being a wonderful exposure to three great characters is also a significant parable that reveals these two truths. Here is my account of that parable.

Whilst initially we painted Melvin as the expert in love we know the reality that he is the obnoxious neighbour, someone to whom Simon justifiably says 'you absolute horror of a human being'.

Even allowing for the dreadful affliction of the OCD, for which neither therapy nor medicines are efficacious, sympathy for Melvin quickly runs out.

His treatment of Simon, the Jews at 'his table', black people, and women in general – with Carol the singular exception, is monstrous and totally unacceptable. He needs to get his act together, but of course Melvin won't see it like that. Or at least he does not at the outset.

And yet Melvin is not without his redeeming features, as inexplicable as these are set against his predominant social conduct.

He takes in Verdell and performs for the muted mutt while sitting at the piano singing, *'Always look on the brighter side of your life'.*

His kindness to Carol is extraordinary and cannot be explained simply by a selfish desire to be waited upon. Melvin doesn't want breakfast, he wants someone to eat breakfast with, including warm rolls at 4 am.

The film clearly seeks out Melvin's redemption, his transformation from obnoxious, multi-phobic, hateful misanthrope into gloriously companionable, generously warm-hearted lover of mankind. The film further points to a repentance by which Melvin chooses to think differently about his life (from which he'd been evicted and to which Simon convinces him never to return).

These twin forces of redemption and repentance are

common themes in Hollywood lore.

But their articulation in this film is singularly impressive in underscoring practical truths that are counter-intuitive and counter-cultural.

A great many people believe that redemption and repentance are fundamental attributes of humankind. These two dynamic forces align themselves with the basic truth that love is the goal, maybe even that love conquers all. They will argue, and I'm happy to go along with this, that morality matters, that truth is vitally important, that love is better than hate and that good is better than evil.

These forces being the underlying conditions for humanity to persevere, with or without there being any purpose to existence, suggests that all people, no matter how bad are capable of being rescued from their plight, and that repentance, a change of mind and of heart, may take place in the most ardent of us.

For me, there is no meaning to life without the personal involvement of a sovereign, unlimitedly merciful God in mankind. I see God's hand at work and his heart on display in this wonderful film. I see his story being told in the lives of Melvin, Carol and Simon and it is a story that blesses all mankind. It is a story in which mankind meets the limits of its ability to control others and itself, and where we find the things that we can't control free us from the need to control. It is a story where when we learn to love ourselves healthily we are released to love others unconditionally. Let us now look again at the story of as good as it gets. We may find it gets even better!

THE LIBERATING COMMUNITY

When we take a closer look at Melvin we see quite clearly a misanthrope who ironically lives a blessed life off the royalties he makes from millions of readers unknown to him, and whom he's happy for them to remain that way. He writes about love and women yet he doesn't know love and he doesn't like women. Yet one woman, Carol, draws him to love.

Melvin is a very poor neighbour – he doesn't like gays and he doesn't care for coloured folk:

'*What colour is that?*' asks Simon –

'*Like molasses!*' says Melvin.

If you're both then you're in a hopeless state. He also doesn't like Latinos judging by his put down of Simon's housekeeper. And yet for all his antipathy towards humankind he gives Simon a room in his home!

Melvin is a very poor customer. Though intensely loyal to one restaurant and one particular waitress, Carol, this can be accounted for by his OCD. He eats alone, uses his own plastic utensils, and is incredibly insensitive to the one woman he wants to wait on him. Yet he helps Carol with her son Spence. Superficially this is so she'll come back to work, but deep down it's because he knows her to be the loadstar of his life.

A peculiar example of his OCD is that Melvin will not step on any cracks in the pavement including those that lie between paving stones. He will go to extraordinary lengths to avoid them producing a weird gate as he meets surprises that cause him to check his step awkwardly. Yet when he finds Verdell, Simon's dog, which he minds while Simon is in hospital, copying this behaviour, he tells him 'Don't you be like me'! That's a crack in Melvin's persona that can let light through.

Now let's look at Carol. The love of Carol's life is her 8-year-old son Spencer who suffers from chronic asthma among many other things most of which don't get diagnosed correctly because the health care she is able to provide for her and her son does not cover adequate testing.

Carol is a great waitress; she is a wonderful listener, very personable, never intrusive, and full of optimism in spite of her son's poor health. She is a single mom, living with her mom, who is disadvantaged when it comes to dating on account of caring for her son. No man is going to come before Spencer.

In a curious way, Spencer is Carol's OCD, cutting her off from love and giving her the answer to the question, 'Is this as good as it gets?' the fatal response, 'Yes!' Yet by entering into a relationship with Melvin the answer to that question from Simon becomes a resounding 'No!'

Finally, let's turn to the last member of this odd trinity, Simon. He is estranged from his parents because his father is disgusted with his sexual orientation, and his mother is too weak to go against her husband.

OCD, an 8-year-old with asthma and parental detestation of homosexuality might seem odd bedfellows but in this movie they are all arresting influences that cause people's lives to be 'as good as it gets'.

Simon barely knows Melvin and does not know Carol at all. But because of a vicious mindless attack on Simon while he is creating a drawing of a client, Simon's life collides in a remarkable way with that of Carol's because of Melvin's unprecedented offer of help to his neighbour.

It is this unplanned, spontaneous, involuntary community of three unrelated, distinctive individuals that proves to be the salvation of each; it is a community that provides a kind of deliverance from bondage where each needs the others to release them from the personal chains that bind.

Melvin needs Carol to be tough with him when he speaks about her son's health with grotesque insensitivity. But Melvin needs her to be tender with him when he tells her 'You make me want to be a better man'. If Melvin has Carol, then life is not 'as good as it gets', it's better. But it takes Simon to enthuse Melvin to go to Carol and tell her that he loves her, that she's the only woman for him, that she completes him. And Simon could not say these things had Melvin not been forced to dog sit Verdell in the first place. Melvin couldn't possibly know that he needed Carol and Simon in his life but when he was faced with that reality he leveraged it and became a better man.

Carol gave Simon a reason to paint again and once and for all settle the issue with his parents. Simon made Carol feel wonderful – 'It was better than sex'. But neither of them would be in that relationship were it not for Melvin who initially involved Carol in the road trip because he was afraid Simon would molest him. None of them are in control; their community controls them to the extent that it made each of them better than as good as it gets.

What is true of Melvin, Carol and Simon is true also of me. I'm as good as it gets until I place myself humbly into a community. It doesn't matter whether it's a golf society, a philosophy class, a hospital radio station, a group of drinkers at a village pub, or a local church. By being part of these communities, it gets better for me. I don't like all of the people in all of these communities, but I've learned to love some of them and that's made me a better man.

I don't want what I am today to be as good as it gets, I want it to be better, and strangely that can't happen on my own, all by myself, and in isolation. It can only happen through belonging. I don't know how it happens and I don't care how it happens. It's not for me to say, it's not for me to control. When I belong, I sort of give up control and that's how it happens. I just know *that* it happens, and I like that. How about you?

THE HEALTHY LOVER

If I may go further, I would now like to give my explanation as to why Melvin was like he is, how he became a changed man, and why this story has a profound truth that is available to each and every one of us.

This is a truth that can set us free, radically change our lives forever, and give us a hunger to search out more truths including those that can be found in the treasure trove of classic movies.

Melvin's basic problem was that he did not like himself.

It ought even be said that he hated himself. Some might say that is because he loved only himself. But Melvin did not love himself. That is the whole point. Let me repeat, **Melvin did not love himself.**

Of course Melvin is selfish, self-centred, egotistical and narcissistic; this is exactly how he appears upon casual observation. However, if you look more deeply into his character, this is a man who hates himself. He hates himself so much that he escapes into a world of fantasy, by writing amazingly successful romantic novels that mean so much to so many readers yet mean nothing to Melvin except a subsequent wealth that insulates him from a society he despises.

It is not easy to love oneself well. It is human nature to love oneself wrongly. The only other option is to not even think about whether loving oneself is a good thing or even an important thing. The problem comes when we consider the injunction 'love your neighbour as you love yourself'. How are we to view this? Some say it could mean 'do unto others as you would be done by'. Fair enough.

The problem is that does not guarantee success. Simon treated Melvin with courtesy, respect, and good grace but he got hostility, contempt and hatred in response. Carol similarly was patient, kind and thoughtful towards Melvin yet he was terse, insensitive and arrogant in his reaction. He went too far once and was pulled up severely and uncompromisingly. He knew it and repented. Is this an example of tough love?

For Carol it was take it or leave it. She could put up with Melvin's plastic knife and fork but not his tactless remark about her son. He had crossed a line. She let him know in no uncertain manner. It was a shock to his system that Melvin needed. Yet still he could not be true to his feelings for her. It was another reason to hate himself.

He needed her back at work not to bring him eggs and

bacon but to bring him salvation, to bring him a redemption he could not articulate because he did not know how to love but which nevertheless he knew he needed. Taking Simon to Baltimore was an excuse he used to continue his therapy under Carol.

But Carol was not willing to be a makeshift therapist to a man too old to be worth the bother of reformation. Only Melvin's insistence that Carol was his only hope would provide the means of engagement. And for Simon to become so emboldened required the clarity, insight and resolution of Simon to be tough with Melvin, lovingly tough, and tell him 'you know who you want', It's inevitable therefore that Melvin should pursue whom he knew he wanted, regardless of any obstacles, including Carol's reluctance to get involved.

In Melvin's final monologue he says:

"I might be the only person on the face of the earth that knows you're the greatest woman on earth. I might be the only one who appreciates how amazing you are in every single thing that you do, and how you are with Spencer, "Spence," and in every single thought that you have, and how you say what you mean, and how you almost always mean something that's all about being straight and good. I think most people miss that about you, and I watch them, wondering how they can watch you bring their food, and clear their tables and never get that they just met the greatest woman alive. And the fact that I get it makes me feel good, about me."

Feeling better about yourself is a step in the right direction to loving yourself well.

Let me be personal at this point. When I look back on my life I find little to love. I have been disloyal, unreliable, unfaithful, selfish, egotistical, and socially hostile. I have been much worse than this. This I know to be my natural state.

When I talk to God about this he does not recognise this description. Not because it is not true but because as true as it was it is now forgotten and forgiven. He now sees me, amazingly and incredibly, as his child.

Loving myself is something I can learn to do when by faith I see myself as God sees me. If God loves me unconditionally and without limit, and if God sees me as his very own beautiful child, how can I do anything other than agree with him, see the same loveliness that God sees in me, and then love myself well?

Seeing myself as God sees me makes me want to be a better man. That's got to be good news for the Simons and the Carols of this world. In fact, news that's as good as it gets.

:

2 PLANES, TRAINS AND AUTOMOBILES

THE HEALTHY LOVER

Neal is an impatient man. His client is being ridiculously indecisive and is putting Neal's schedule at risk. Neal is booked and ticketed first class on the United Airlines 6pm flight back home to Chicago. He is looking forward to spending Thanksgiving with his family. He has been working exceedingly hard since the summer holidays without a break and he's now looking for a restful long weekend at home. His client is not his friend right now.

Neal is a hotshot marketing executive, at the top of his profession. He didn't get there by being indecisive. He reached the summit by being focussed, fearless and, relatively friendless. He turns to his colleague and intimates that time is running out. Is there anything John can do to speed things up and help this ludicrously stupid client come to a decision about Neal's brilliant marketing strategy? His colleague is in no hurry. He's not on the 6. Maybe he's decided to overnight in Manhattan and see the town, live a little, and take advantage of their company's expense account? Maybe he'll just do those things that Neal has eschewed for the love of his family. His colleague is not his friend right now.

The mansion back in Chicago is huge with 6 bedrooms and a guest apartment over the garage. For the weekend it will be home to Neal, his wife, their three young kids, Neal's parents and his wife's parents. It sits at the head of a long tree-lined avenue of fabulous homes that seem to form a guard of honour to a royal residence that befits a marketing guru. Neal has been spending a lot of time on the road, in the air, away from his family, and he knows it. His plan is simple: make the 6, get back to Chicago for 7, be home by 8, kiss the kids good night and enjoy cocktails with the adults. Time is not his friend right now.

The meeting ends with no decision. Neal makes a dash for the elevator and realises he's left his gloves behind. That's OK. John will get them and return them to him back in Chicago. It's simple: Neal gets out the building, into a cab, through the terminal at JFK, onto a plane, out of O'Hare, into his car, onto his driveway, and then into the arms of his adoring wife. He won't need his gloves even though it is late November, there's snow on the ground, and a storm is pushing through the North Eastern USA. He will not be deterred. His plan is his friend right now.

Rush hour in Manhattan makes hailing a taxi problematic. Finally, a white light is spotted atop the yellow cab. That's the one for Neal. Across the street a competitor is spotted. A race is signalled and the gun goes off. Down the streets rush the two pedestrians towards the white light. Neal wins. Of course – that's what he does. But wait! A third-party steps in at the last minute. The cab is the property of this undetected interloper. If Neal loses this cab, he won't make the 6 and his plan is ruined. Time to make a deal. Here's how that goes:

"Sir? Sir, excuse me. I know this is your cab, but I'm desperately late for a plane, and I was wondering if I could appeal to your good nature and ask you to let me have it."

"I don't have a good nature. Excuse me."

"Can I offer you ten dollars for it?"

"Nah."

"Twenty! I'll give you twenty dollars for it."

"I'll take fifty."

"All right, all right."

"Anyone who'd pay fifty dollars for a cab... would certainly pay seventy-five."

"Not necessarily... All right, seventy-five dollars. You're a thief!"

"Close. I'm an attorney."

"Have a happy holiday."

"This'll help."

The cab is now Neal's but while he was bargaining for it, a large man with an even larger suitcase is loading the baggage into the trunk of the cab and climbing into the back seat. Having paid the merciless attorney his ill-gotten gains, Neal is now confused as to why his cab is pulling off with someone else in it. His hot pursuit of the disappearing cab is all in vain. That passenger is not his friend right now.

Amazingly Neal gets another cab and this time does not have to pay an extortionate fee to a lawyer or anyone else for the privilege. He makes it to JFK and rushes to the gate. He is going to make the 6. But the weather is not his friend right now.

The 6 is delayed – indefinitely. Neal calls home and reports the flight delay. He is still hopeful of kissing his kids goodnight and will certainly be in time for cocktails. His wife is sceptical. She'll wait up though.

Neal waits in the overcrowded gate area and settles

down to read a magazine article that his friend wrote. Opposite him is the mystery cab thief. He is reading a paperback with the dubious title 'The Canadian Mounted'. Neal ponders on taking the thief to task but decides to let it go. However, Neal's staring at the cab thief has drawn the paperback reader's attention. The large man puts his book down and starts a conversation:

"I know you, don't I? I'm usually very good with names but I'll be darned if I haven't forgotten yours."

"You stole my cab."

"I never stole anything in my life."

"I hailed a cab on Park Avenue this afternoon and before I could get in it. You stole it."

"You're the guy who tried to get my cab. I knew I knew you! You scared the daylights out of me. Come to think of it, it was easy to get a cab during rush hour."

"Forget it."

"I can't forget it. I am sorry. I had no idea it was your cab. Let me make it up to you. How about a nice hot dog and a beer?"

"No thanks."

"Just a hot dog then."

"I'm kinda picky about what I eat."

"Some coffee?"

"No."

"Milk?"

"No."

Neal's annoyance is rising. This guy is not his friend.

"Soda?"

"No."

"Tea?"

"No"

"LifeSavers?"

"No."

"Slurpee?"

"Sir - please."

"Just let me know. I'm here. I knew I knew ya!"

The flight is called, the 6 has become the 8, but at least it's first class all the way home now. Oh dear, there's more bad news for Neal!

Although he was booked and ticketed over 3 months ago in first class his mistakenly issued boarding pass puts him in coach and what is even worse, he is seated next to the cab thief. The airline is not his friend right now.

The car thief is pleased to renew his acquaintance with Neal and introduces himself as Del. He has no wish to be an annoying blabbermouth, so he sleeps, his socks in hand, perched on the aisle seat hemming Neal in between himself and the old gentleman snoring soundly in the window seat.

Coach is not first class and life is distinctly unfair but this grotesque inconvenience is just about bearable for the hop over the Adirondacks to the Windy City. Except the storm that caused the flight delay has worsened and they are now headed for Wichita, Kansas where every aircraft that lands there will be stranded for the night.

Neal is stuck in Wichita with nowhere to stay because all the beds are taken, unsurprisingly, given the massive disruption the storm has caused. Neal's abandoned gloves may prove significant at this time, but Neal is more afraid of losing his mind. The storm is not his friend right now. It is Tuesday.

I LIKE ME

Del is a congenial guy. His job for American Light and Fixtures is Sales Director in the shower curtain rings division. His customers like him, his wife likes him and as he says, 'I like me'. That may sound strange and possibly even narcissistic but what Del means is that he is comfortable in his own skin. He is saying he does not feel the need to change and the way he is appeals to lots of other people. Del knows lots of people and has made lots of friends, but he also has a secret. He has told no one this secret and keeping it limits his freedom. It may be that he will never be free until he tells his secret but whomever he tells, he must be convinced that person is a true friend.

Words that capture the essence of Del include sociable, joyful, optimistic, resilient and principled. He is as folk say 'the salt of the earth'. He would have been mortified by the accusation that he stole someone's cab. But he knew he had made an error in Neal's case and he wanted to make it up to him. Now was his chance.

The Braidwood Inn is off the beaten track. You wouldn't happen by it unless you made it your destination, and this is not the kind of location Neal would load into his sat nav. Neal is more of a Hyatt Regency person. But when Del suggests he may be able to find a room for Neal, because he is well known to Gus the manager there, Neal is willing to humble himself this one time. Neal has keenly observed the blanket of sleeping humanity covering the entire floor area in the airport terminal and he's with Del.

The trip to the Inn is courtesy of Doobie's taxis and Doobie himself insists on taking the slow roads to show off his town. 'You don't see nothing on the Interstate but Interstate' he asserts. Indeed, but it is the middle of the night Doobie – possibly the best time to see Wichita!

Gus is able to come up with a special deal for the hapless pair – the last room in the complex, a double. Neal is horrified at the prospect of sharing a room with Del but the situation becomes even more spine chilling when the pair realise there is just the one bed. The nightmare is about to begin.

Dell is not the tidiest of guys. When it's Neal's turn to use the shower, he finds the bathroom littered with wet towels and detritus. Del's socks and underwear are in the sink. Neal offers his weary body to the trickle of water and gazes wistfully at the shower curtain rings. There's really no getting away from 'this guy'. His only means to dry himself is with a small washcloth.

Del meanwhile is clean and contented. He experiments with the waterbed while drinking beer and smoking a cigarette. A framed photograph of his wife Marie, which he carries with him wherever he travels, is lovingly placed on the nightstand. He may be unable to sleep with her but he can bid her good night.

After the reluctant bedfellows turn out the light, sleep unfortunately does not immediately follow. Del must clear out his sinuses. It has a dissonant musical quality but this is no opera Neal is willing to endure. He finally snaps, leaps out of bed in an uncontrolled rage and furiously unleashes a scathing tirade on Del. The bemused shower curtain ring guy wants to know what he's done wrong – again, when all he has done is to fix Neal up with a bed for the night. Listen to some of the pent-up abuse that is exchanged between the two:

"Without clearing my sinuses, I'll snore all night. If your kid spills his milk, do you slap him?"

"What-what-what is that supposed to mean?"

"You're not a very tolerant person."

"You've bugged me since New York, starting with stealing my cab."

"My oh my you're a mean dude."

"How would you like a mouthful of teeth?"

"Oh, and hostile, too. Nice personality combination-- hostile and intolerant. That's borderline criminal."

"What about you? You spill beer all over the bed, you mess up the bathroom..."

"Who let you stay? I even let you pay, so you wouldn't feel like an intruder."

"An intruder? Right."

"You ruined a nice trip."

"Who talked my ear off on the plane? Who was that? I'm curious."

"Who told you to book a room? I did. You're an ungrateful jackass. Sleep in the lobby. I hope you wake up so stiff you can't even move."

And now Neal goes for the kill:

"You're no saint. You got a free cab, you got a free room and someone who'll listen to your boring stories. I mean didn't you notice on the plane when you started talking, eventually I started reading the vomit bag? Didn't that give you some sort of clue, like, hey, maybe this guy's not enjoying it?

You know, everything is not an anecdote. You have to discriminate. You choose things that are funny or mildly amusing or interesting. You're a miracle! Your stories have none of that. They're not even amusing, *accidentally*!

"Honey I'd like you to meet Del Girffith, he's got some amusing anecdotes for you. Oh, and here's a gun so you can blow your brains out. You'll thank me for it"

I could tolerate any insurance seminar. For days. I could sit there and listen to them go on and on with a big smile on my face. They'd say "How can you stand it?" I'd say "'Cause I've been with Del Griffith. I can take anything." You know what they'd say? They'd say "I know what you mean. The shower curtain ring guy. Whoa"

It's like going on a date with a Chatty Cathy doll. I expect you have a little string on your chest, you know, that I pull our and have to snap back. Except I wouldn't pull it out and snap it back, you would. Agh! Agh! Agh! Agh!

And by the way, you know, when you're telling these little stories. Here's a good idea; have a point. It makes it so much more interesting for the listener!"

I don't know about you but if I suffered such a verbal onslaught I'd be mortally wounded. But Del is made of sterner stuff. He knows who he is and he likes himself. Here's a noble response from a guy who makes a meagre living selling shower curtain rings:

"You wanna hurt me? Go right ahead if it makes you feel any better. I'm an easy target. Yeah you're right, I talk too much. I also listen too much. I could be a cold-hearted cynic like you… but I don't like to hurt people's feelings. Well, you think what you want about me; I'm not changing. I like me. My wife likes me. My customers like me. 'Cause I'm the real article. What you see is what you get."

Bravo Del. What are you going to do now Neal, you ungrateful, stuck up, affluent, friendless prig? The answer to that is climb back into bed where sleep inevitably has its way with the oddest of couple. And while they slumber a thief breaks in undetected and helps himself to the contents of their wallets.

When it comes time to pay for breakfast they discover their loss. Neal once again accuses Del of being a thief. When it's clear that Del's wallet has been emptied also they finally have something in common - an unknown robber.

Now they must also share a common goal – an improvised trip to Chicago, a journey of some 700 miles, 10 hours by car. All the flights are either cancelled or fully booked. The storm has created a major disturbance at exactly the time when most of America is on the move to be with family. It is Wednesday.

YOU'RE GOING THE WRONG WAY

The temperature in Kansas around Thanksgiving can fall below zero Fahrenheit. That is cold. Del's luggage contains clothes for all climes, from a Wisconsin winter to a Floridian Fall. Neal is less well prepared. His gloves were abandoned in New York. Neal's wardrobe adorns his dressing room in the Chicago mansion. Neal's planning has hardly been his friend, but Del could become his friend if Neal is smart enough to let him in.

Neal's Visa card and Del's network of contacts are a

powerful combination. Two train tickets are secured but
unfortunately, they are seated in separate cars. Neal doesn't
mind. As in MLK's dream, he is 'free at last', except the train
breaks down, as the mishaps continue.

The stranded passengers are told to make their way
across one of the millions of acres of farmland in Kansas to
a coach that will ferry them to the bus depot where they can
then ride into St Louis, about halfway to where they are
headed. The odyssey begins.

When Neal sees Del struggling to drag his luggage across
the field he goes to his aid. His freedom has been short
lived. His time with Del is not yet ended. There is more that
Neal can learn from Del but is he up for it?

Upon reaching the great state of Missouri, Del realises
that he is sitting on hidden gold. In his luggage, Del carries
many samples of shower curtain rings to show customers.
Using his incomparable sales patter, Del can easily convert
these to cash by selling them as designer earrings to
impressionable young teen girls. His entire stock is traded
for a couple of hundred dollars cash. Neal acknowledges
this salesmanship. Del thinks the two of them make a great
team but Neal isn't ready to play ball.

Neal has tried to call home but no one is answering. The
family are probably at the daughter's Thanksgiving pageant,
family events not to be missed that are never repeated.

Neal confesses that he's been spending too much time
at work. He sees how he has got his priorities wrong. In
working hard to provide for his family he has missed seeing
his family.

Del admits he hadn't been home in years. When Neal
challenges him on this Del walks it back as 'Just a figure of
speech'. Del is holding on to his secret.

He tells Neal, 'I got a motto – like your work, love your
wife'. That rings so true for Neal who is now wondering if
it is true for Del then how come he hasn't 'been home in

years' – literally or figuratively.

But Neal isn't about to pursue that line of interrogation right now. His goal is to get home. And that means jettisoning Del who is crestfallen to hear the news that a budding relationship is being cut short.

Del, wounded and hurt, tips up half of his cash gained from hustling shower curtain rings as teenage earrings. He makes an impromptu, sorrowful departure leaving the marketing guru to his own devices. This journey is now about to turn into a marathon. It is still Wednesday.

Neal rents a car from Marathon Rentals at St Louis airport. Unfortunately, when the courtesy bus drops him off at the designated location the lot is vacant. Neal is incandescent. He makes his way back to the terminal and the car rental booth on foot, in the freezing cold, across runways from which fully loaded planes take off carrying Americans home for the holidays. When he gets to the head of the line, he lets rip at the assistant who is unable to help because Neal has lost his rental agreement. He is about to lose his mind. The end of this nightmare is not yet insight. It is late Wednesday evening.

Del has been driving while Neal sleeps. It is Interstate 55 all the way now and there's still time to make it home for Thanksgiving dinner but the misadventures are by no means over.

Del tries to take his coat off while driving, always a dangerous manoeuvre. He gets his Parka snarled up in the seat adjustment lever and in trying to wrestle it free, loses control of the vehicle and veers off I-55 down an off ramp, bringing the car, now turned around, to a halt. Forgetfully, Del now proceeds up the off ramp and is headed back along I-55 towards St Louis on the wrong side of the freeway. They are going the wrong way TWICE over!!

A couple on the other side of the freeway shout and scream 'You're going the wrong way' but the odd couple reason 'How would they know which way we're going' and conclude that the alarm is a consequence of drunkenness.

Neal and Del realise their error when two oncoming oversized lorries confront them. It's too late to make those wills!

Amazingly the car escapes through the narrow gap between the oncoming trucks scraping both sides of the vehicle along its entire length. It's a tight squeeze – and it's still not over.

The pair get out, and while they engage in an argument, the car bursts into flames with the ensuing fire turning their wallets into ashes. When the flames go out the car incomprehensively can still be driven to a nearby motel. Neither have sufficient funds to pay for a room. Neal has $17 and a heck of a nice watch, which covers his admission. Del has a few cents and a Casio. He's left outside freezing in the wreckage of the car. As the snow falls, Del muses to himself:

"Well Marie, once again my dear, you were as right as rain. I am, without doubt, the biggest pain in the neck that ever came down the pike. I meet someone whose company I really enjoy and what do I do? I go overboard. I smother the poor soul. I cause him more trouble that he has a right to. My, do I have a big mouth! When am I ever gonna wake up? I wish you were here with me right now. But… I guess that's not gonna happen. Not now, anyway."

Neal is restless in his warm bed while a fellow human being suffers outside, so mercifully he relents and calls Del in. The two of them party using the contents of the motel's mini-bar. After trips to sample the liquor from Italy, Mexico and Jamaica they philosophise:

"You know, when I'm dead and buried, all I'm gonna have around here to prove that I was here are some shower curtain rings that didn't fall down. Great legacy, huh?"

"At the very least, the absolute minimum, you've got a woman you love to grow old with, right? You love her, don't you?"

"Love... is not a big enough word. It's not a big enough word for how I feel about my wife."

"To the wives."

"To the wives!"

It looks like Neal has a new friend. Del still has a secret. It is Thursday.

I'D LIKE YOU TO MEET A FRIEND OF MINE

As if by a miracle the two weary travellers are finally back in Chicago saying their fond farewells at the METRA train station on the commuter rail system that serves the city's suburbs. Neal goes first:

"It's been a heck of a trip."

"Sure has."

"But, uh, after all is said and done, you did get me home."

"Next time, let's go first class, all right?"

"I hope there isn't a next time."

"I know. This you?" (Neal's train is arriving).

"Yeah. It's been great meeting you."

"I'm sorry if I caused you any trouble."

"You got me home, and, uh... a little late."

"A couple of days."

"But, uh... I'm a little wiser, too."

"Me, too."

"Happy holidays."

"Same to you. Happy Thanksgiving, Neal. Give my love to the family. Maybe I'll meet them someday."

"Say hello to Marie for me."

"Yeah."

"So...OK. And you have a happy Thanksgiving."

"Hey, you know it."

"So long."

Neal is finally free of Del. He has a new friend who he'll never see again. Del has a secret that he'll keep to himself until he finds that true friend. Del drags his luggage to the waiting room. What is he waiting for?

As the only passenger on the train Neal is alone with his thoughts. He can with immunity recall the past 48 hours. The underwear in the sink; his tirade at Del; his missing watch which was the price of admission to the motel last night; the drinks party; the toast to the wives. To the wives. The wives? Del hasn't been home in years. Why not? What is wrong? There's something not right. Something very extraordinary and utterly remarkable is about to happen.

For 48 hours, come what may, Neal has been trying to get home to his family. He has been wearing the same underwear since Tuesday. He has scraped through a near fatal collision. He has been on his last legs. He is on the last leg. He is on the train that will carry him to the home he has had as his goal for 48 hours. He gets off the train!
Let me say that again in case you missed it. He gets off the train that is taking him home. He now gets on another empty train going away from his home. A train that is going back to the station where he left Del. Where he now finds Del.
Del is seated silent and forlorn. He looks up at his new friend. The new friend who has returned. Is he the true friend?
"Del, what are you doing here? You said you were going home, what are you doing here?"
"I uh... I don't have a home. Marie's been dead for eight years."

As Neal and Del walk along the tree-lined avenue of

fabulous homes towards the royal residence they each have a hand on Del's heavy bag. Del is carrying Neal's briefcase. Neal is carrying Del's other luggage. They are sharing their burdens.

Del has unloaded one of his massive burdens. He has told the truth about Marie. He has revealed the secret of her passing. He has made himself vulnerable. He has safely entrusted himself into the arms of a true friend.

Neal who has made few friends having disregarded so many opportunities to do so, thinking of others as hostile is a little wiser as he puts it. In fact he has underestimated his progress. He is MUCH wiser.

The two of them are almost home. Del is overwhelmed by the majesty of the family residence that he sees as he draws closer. Few words are needed between true friends:

"Boy, you are one lucky guy, Neal."

"I know."

"I won't stay long. Maybe I'll just say 'Hi', then be on my way."

"Just come on."

The door to the family home is flung open. There are screams of delight. Smiles light up on the sea of faces. Neal makes some introductions:

Del Griffith, meet my father-in-law Walt, my mother-in-law Peg, my mother Joy, and my dad Martin.

"Welcome, Del."

This little guy's Neal Jr., my little gem Marti, and somewhere around here is my baby boy Seth.

Neal's wife is at the back of the line. But the last shall be first right?

"Honey, I'd like you to meet a friend of mine."

"Hello, Mr Griffith"

"Hello, Mrs Page."

Good job Neal. Welcome to the family Del.

THE PICTURE'S PARABLE

The story of Neal and Del is of course brilliantly told in the 1987 film *Planes, Trains and Automobiles* which was written, directed and produced by John Hughes.

The film awards community overwhelmingly disregarded this picture despite endearing performances by Steve Martin (Neal Page) and John Candy (Del Griffith). This unwarranted disinterest does nothing however to detract from the greatness of the film.

I have watched it multiple times and I always cry at the end. I laugh throughout the film, but I always shed tears at the end, even though I know what is coming. I think I know every word of dialogue, every facial expression and every bit of background music. It is a brilliant film because I have discovered that enduring truths are the source of its brilliance.

Jesus, who I think is one of the best storytellers every, maybe even the greatest, would own this story. That is because it is all about the meaning of friendship, a subject about which he spoke at length.

Of course it is also a story of redemption. Neal ceases his arrogance, and Del stops covering up the death of his wife to protect himself from a pitied existence. These two characters find each other and so find themselves.

There are two eternal verities that the film makes. The first is that sometimes our world must be turned upside down in order for us to be able to see the right way up. The second is that the truth sets us free.

The film can rightly be included in my list of Hollywood parables and I'd like to amplify why this is.

Neal has a perfectly ordered world. We don't know

much about his past but my guess is that he was a well-behaved child who learned from his parents, Martin and Joy, the meaning of obedience, industry, civility and duty. He performed well at school, probably excelling academically. He was a capable athlete – we know he could sprint because of the cab incident. He graduated from college, very likely with honours, and then got himself on the professional ladder by joining a major corporation. He was rapidly promoted by being industrious, ambitious, cooperative and smart. He was at the top of his game.

He married a beautiful woman and they are blessed with three wonderful children. The family home easily accommodates both sets of grandparents at Thanksgiving. It is house both large and welcoming. Neal's world is a success story. He is living the American dream - until a nightmare wakes him up.

He flies first class where neither Slurpee nor hotdog is served, only champagne and canapés. You meet a better kind of fake in first.

Neal's friends are few and they are well chosen. They are filtered through a strainer of his careful design, one that matches his own values and priorities. It is simple to prevent undesired objects from passing through this filter be it a client, a colleague, a cab thief, a flight attendant or the weather god – whoever she is.

Neal's world is made to his design where order matters. He is on the throne of his life. His royal residence in one of Chicago's wealthiest suburbs is a symbol of his kingdom. None of this makes Neal a bad person – far from it. Neal is a good person. It just means that Neal is the one who decides what is good and bad.

When disorder invades this world Neal is unhappy, confused and resistant. At first it is little things like an indecisive client, a thieving attorney, a cab hijacker, and an errant ticket supervisor. But the trickle of disorder turns into a deluge with an unprecedented winter storm. This now represents more than an unrelated series of unjust inconveniences; this is, by Neal's reckoning, hostile action waged by an invisible enemy, witness his outburst at the car rental lot.

As I see it, this tsunami of grief is indeed purposeful but in fact it is a deliberate disruption that is inverting Neal's world so that he can see things differently, but all of this needs time to take effect.

In saying his farewells Neal made clear that he was a 'little wiser'. He underestimates his progress. He is much wiser. Look at a couple of major learning points: first, that money can't solve problems; and secondly, that connecting with people rather than condemning them is what makes life sweeter. A closer inspection of these leads to a re-evaluation of life's priorities.

Let's look at money in the movie. Neal 'buys' a cab off an avaricious attorney yet it is taken from him by an innocent simpleton. Moments later Neal gets another cab 'for free'. Much good the $75 brought!

He has paid for a first-class ticket, which cost a bomb, yet Neal is issued with an incorrect boarding pass for a seat in coach. It must rate as the most expensive, least comfortable airplane ride of his life thus far.

A thief empties his wallet of cash in the night while he sleeps with a strange man. Who exactly is in control here, please remind me?

His credit cards get incinerated while he can only look on helplessly. He has to barter for a $70 room with a $7000 watch.

What exactly is the value of money?

A Hollywood celebrity once said, 'I've been poor and

I've been rich, and rich is better'. I get it. But there must be a great many film stars who would trade their wealth for lasting peace and real happiness.

Disorder taught Neal something about money that his financial advisers never did. He was not wrong in wanting the very best for his family and working exceedingly hard to provide for their every need. But when it comes to choosing between a cheque book or a cuddle there should be only one winner. It's all about priorities, and to get those right it matters on your perspective.

Let's look at people in the movie. In rough order of appearance there is the client, the colleague, the attorney, the cab thief (Del), the flight attendant, the guy in the window seat, the thief in the night, the Marathon Car Rental counter attendant, the cab despatcher, and then there was, as always, Del.

All of the above are uncooperative dissidents. They are unjust inconveniences. They are unwanted obstacles. They are incompliant intruders. All of this is true from a particular point of view.

And then atop them all there is Del. And Del said:

'I got a motto - like your work, love your wife'

Del spoke and Neal heard. Neal had been reading the vomit bag on the plane when Del had been droning on as the aircraft was diverted. But Neal was listening now. Now everything changed. He would not be diverted. Neal's point of view got inverted. Neal can now give thanks for everyone of these people and count them a blessing; strident signposts that shouted 'Look this way Neal'.

He can regard these people no longer as obstacles wreaking disorder but as instruments of an invisible re-ordering of Neal's priorities, and of a silent reorienting of Neal's outlook.

There is a verse in the Bible that says:
Consider it pure joy ... -whenever you face trials of many kinds

Yeah, right! Good luck with that. It is of course humanly impossible. The reason for this is because it challenges us to take a fresh look at the world we have arranged for ourselves and we are naturally reluctant to change the way we think and the way we look at life. We reasonably believe that the way we view life is correct and how we arrange our lives to suit this view is in our best interests. The reality is that this is almost certainly not so.

Believe it or not, God has our very best interests at heart because he loves us unconditionally and limitlessly. This is why he wants to order our world because his arrangement is infinitely better than anything we could come up with. When we go along with him, he brings about a reordering process using 'trials of many kinds'. He sets up a new worldview and a new response system that is perfectly matched with our best interests.

Neal's world got reordered when he committed himself to a new way of living for and with his family.

And miraculously he would include in this family this unsociable shower curtain ring salesman with a large luggage case and an even larger heart.

I know for sure that Neal heard what Del said, because he got off the train that was taking him home, he then got on a train that took him away from home in order that he could find someone that had no home so that he could give him a home, and all because Del had already found a home in Neal's heart.

This parable is nourishment to our souls. That's why it's a great movie.

FREEDOM AND FRIENDSHIP

There is a piece of wisdom in the Bible that goes something like this .....

Two are better than one, because they have a good return for their labour: If either of them falls down, one can help the other up. But pity anyone who falls and has no one to help him or her up. Also, if two lie down together, they will keep warm, but how can one keep warm alone?

It reminds me of the scene in the film where Del is cuddling Neal in bed. It is the day before Thanksgiving. They are stuck in Kansas. It is bitterly cold outside. Maybe the room was not heated overnight – it's better that way. The bed offers some warmth but two people cuddled together offer greater warmth.

This world can be a cold place. If you're all on your own it can be a tough world and a bitter one – bitterly cold. If complete strangers can become friends they bring each other warmth to overcome the cold. Togetherness brings warmth and so each is made to feel better because the other is part of their world.

I make no judgment on two men, complete strangers, cuddling one another and being horrified when they realise their predicament. The correctness or otherwise of their intermixing and sudden separation has little do with the principle that this wisdom piece shows us.

It is a principle that has been underscored by the global pandemic that Covid-19 inflicted on the world – 'no-one is safe until everyone is safe'.

If two people are in a boat that has a hole in it that lets the water gush through threatening to drown the occupants, the one can take no comfort that the hole is at the other person's end! It helps though there are two to bail.

For many people their view of God is that he is angry, disappointed or disinterested. God is a judge, he knows my faults and holds me accountable for them. This is not someone I can cuddle. Once I believed in such a God, but not anymore. The God in whom I believe will get into my bed and let me cuddle him. His judgement of me is tempered by the truth that he loves me unconditionally and limitlessly. He is my heavenly Father and he is my friend.

What is a friend? He or she is someone I love to spend time with, someone I want to get to know better, to whom I listen intently when they speak, and to whom I can talk freely and openly. A friend is someone to whom I am unafraid to reveal the truth about myself because I know I won't be judged. I will be understood and be comforted. My God is such a friend.

A scene that paints another false view of God is when Neal leaves Del behind and heads for home. Neal is relieved to be rid of Del. There will never be a 'next time'. Neal is going home to be with his family. It is his home where his children live; it is open only to members of his family and closed to all others.

So many people see God as having 'his own' gathered to himself and 'the others' shut out – left to their loneliness and their homelessness. That is a horrible view of God and an utterly false one. My God is the Neal that gets off the train and goes looking for Del. My God goes looking for the lost sheep and the lost coin. My God keeps a look out for the lost son.

Neal got off the train that was taking him home and got on a train that took him back to Del because he knew in his soul that something was wrong. Neal found Del and asked 'What are you doing here; you said you were going home?'

Then came a moment of truth for Del, would he continue the deception about Marie or would he confess? Was he surprised to see Neal, perhaps even stunned? Might it be that this two-day-old affair was the beginning of something enduring and real, maybe even everlasting? Was Neal the person that Del had been waiting for to tell the truth that Marie was dead and that he was homeless?

The Bible speaks about the truth setting us free. God asks *'Are you alone? Are you homeless? Are you friendless? Are you weary?'* He of course knows the answer to all these questions and he asks them not so that he can pity us, mock us, or judge us. He asks so that he then can offer us a home and a friend. He offers himself.

Jesus, who brought God's message of good news of friendship, said something like this: *'Greater love has no man than this, that he lays down his life for his friends'.*

And that is what Jesus did, that is how he showed us he is our friend.

In a beautiful, symbolic sense that is what Neal did. He got off the train taking him home, laying down temporarily the occupation of his royal residence and foregoing the sight of his family, in order to show an extraordinary friendship to Del.

He headed for Del to free him from the guilt of his concealment and the fear of being pitied. An undeserved and wholly unexpected freedom became Del's, the freedom of the royal residence and the companionship of a family that said, 'Welcome, Del'.

This royal welcome had been foreshadowed earlier in the film when Neal paid for the motel on Wednesday evening. He gave up an expensive watch and his last few dollars to secure the shelter from the winter storm.

And then, unexpectedly and quite remarkably he shared the room with someone who could not pay for it himself.

And the two friends partied all around the world!

I don't know how long Del stayed or whether he ever returned. But he lived the rest of his days knowing that he could do so whenever he needed to and was part of that family forever.

Neal and Del were blessed with a friendship forged in

adversity. Their story is a parable for the sufferings and death of Jesus on the cross that leads to an eternal friendship between all humankind and their divine creator.

I'm so pleased Neal didn't go back for his gloves.

3 SPARTACUS

YOU DON'T WANT TO KNOW MY NAME

His fellow man had fallen, what else could he do but come to his aid? He squatted down and released himself from his own heavy load. Next, he went to his fallen neighbour and released him from the basket of heavy stones that had been too much of a burden for him to carry. The load had crushed him as he suffered under the sun that baked the wilderness where the slaves laboured incessantly.

The rescuer offered the fallen man a drink, lifting the water bottle to parched lips. A Roman soldier dashes the bottle from his hand spilling its precious contents on the rocky path the slaves tread from quarry to loading bays. Then the Roman set about beating the fallen man for failing to do his job and extended the beating to the rescuer, a younger stronger man with greater fight than his fellow slave. The beatings are indiscriminate, the one for weakness in body, the other for strength of character.

The rescuer takes a bite out of the soldier's leg, sinking a perfect set of teeth into the Roman's hamstring. More soldiers come to the aid of their comrade and punish his assailant severely for this unpardonable violation. The rescuer will no longer be required to be a burden bearer for others or himself. He is fastened to a stake to be left to die with neither food nor water exposed to the searing sun that beats down from a cloudless blue sky.

There are plenty more slaves to work the mine for materials. Putting men to death is just a part of Roman imperialism in the cause of bringing civilisation to a chaotic world. The rescuer is a forgettable casualty, yet one more dispensable commodity. His death will serve as a reminder of Roman justice and an unambiguous warning to others who would rebel. His name is Spartacus.

Batiatus is scouring the mine for his own materials. Carried along in his palanquin by four personal slaves he is looking for worthy specimens of flesh, blood and bone, strong young men capable of being trained for his business.

Batiatus is the owner of a gladiator school. He recognises a bargain when he sees one. Spartacus has good muscle tone, confirmed by the gentle sweep of a fan across the chest. His teeth are also in first-rate condition, a sure sign of a healthy specimen

'*As the teeth go so also do the bones*' says Batiatus to the Roman soldier who will be glad to be rid of an annoying troublemaker for a pocketful of denarii.

Spartacus will make a useful addition to his commercial enterprise. He will be fed, watered, accommodated, exercised and trained. When he is ready, he will be exhibited in various circuses as a spectacle for the mindless pleasure of wealthy Romans.

Spartacus is a proud, rebellious, young man, born into slavery in a conquered Thracian household, sold into a living death in the mines of Libya, unable to dream of the death of slavery, and now transposed into the confined freedom of a school for gladiators. It is a school whose pupils are destined to die, at some stage or other, in a barbaric sport intended to satisfy the sadistic desires of corrupt Roman imperialists. No longer a slave, he is free to die for the entertainment of his former slave owners. For a slave, death is freedom.

The chief coach in the school is Marcellus. He was once a gladiator but was graciously granted his freedom by Batiatus because he outlasted all his peers. It is an example of success that encourages all gladiators to aspire. Win your fights, defeat your opponents, acquire expertise and reputation, and free yourself by being the best. The losers find their freedom in death. The victors become better athletes, the competition becomes fiercer, the entertainment value of contests is enhanced, and the crowds are more delighted. It is a shrewd business model that brings Batiatus fame and fortune.

It is also a cynical evolutionary process that thrives on killing off your competitors, outlasting other victors, and ensuring the survival of the fittest. But Spartacus refuses to mutate into a Marcellus. He sees into his trainer's soul and despises what he finds. Likewise, Marcellus knows the newcomer to be an intransigent and capable of challenging his own position. The two of them recognise in the other a potential threat. This brooding hostility will bubble over later into a radical revolution, one driven by the dream of Spartacus to free every Roman slave and put slavery to death. In the meanwhile, Imperialism thrives with slavery its servant.

On one occasion, a group of Roman dignitaries visit the school while celebrating the engagement to be married of two of their party. The leader of this group is Crassus, a person of great renown. He is a Senator of Rome, commander of a private army of many legions, a considerably wealthy landowner, and an aristocrat with an ancestry that dates back to the foundation of Rome herself.

His wife Helena has decided to make an engagement gift to her brother Marcus and his new fiancé Claudia. That gift is a spectacle in which two pairs of gladiators in turn will fight to the death.

Marcus is a protégé of Crassus who makes him the gift of the garrison of Rome in respect of him becoming his brother-in-law. This is another part of the plan that Crassus has to restore patrician governance to Rome, replacing what he sees as the corrupt rule of the republican Senate with an effective dictatorship.

Batiatus escorts the party to view the gladiators so that Helena and Claudia can choose who will fight. In one of the pairings, Spartacus is pitted against a black giant, perhaps the most skilled of the entire group.

Spartacus recalls his failed attempt to make conversation with the giant in his early days. It is telling for its brevity and poignancy. Spartacus begins:

"What's your name?"

"You don't want to know my name. I don't want to know your name."

"Just a friendly question."

"Gladiators don't make friends. If we're ever matched in the arena together, I have to kill you."

The black giant has spoken. He now sits in silence with Spartacus as the two wait their turn to fight. They watch another pair of fellow gladiators. Crixus is the victor; his opponent lies dead in the arena. The Romans are entertained. The next pair is called to perform – Spartacus versus the man with no name.

Now the black giant will do his talking with net and trident while Spartacus has a short sword and shield. The visiting party engage in idle chatter almost oblivious to the two human beings below them fighting for their freedom.

The contest is close. The black giant may have thought it would be straightforward to vanquish the recent addition to the school, but he would have taken nothing for granted. That is just as well because Spartacus fights with skill and determination. He is no friend of the giant but in different circumstances he would be. The two muscular specimens struggle for supremacy in the baking sun while the women fantasise about how they will celebrate with the victor.

Finally, the giant pins Spartacus to the floor. He has the prostrate novice at his mercy. It is for Helena, the wife of Crassus, to determine the fate of the defeated Spartacus. The giant is breathless from his contest and has pity on his foe. His sweating face bears a look that pleads for mercy.

The contest was keenly fought; neither man gives an inch or expects any from the other. The result could have gone either way. The Romans have been well and truly entertained. Mercy is a reasonable outcome. No more death is required, at least from any rational observer.

Helena gives the thumbs down, the sign that Spartacus is to have his life extinguished. So must be the fate of all those vanquished by Rome.

The black giant, his face soaked in perspiration, looks at the man whose name he did not wish to know and against whose neck he now holds the tips of the trident's tines. Spartacus closes his eyes expecting to see a different world when they reopen. There is one last glance to the woman, her thumb stubbornly fixed downwards. She is resolute, but so also the victor.

He stands to his feet and runs towards the gallery throwing his trident as he approaches the spectators in the hope of killing or wounding one of them. It misses them all. He continues his ludicrous assault. Leaping up high, he grabs the edge of the gallery on which the Roman party is seated. A soldier hurls his spear, which strikes the gladiator in the back, mortally wounding the foolish assailant.

A noble gesture to make a stand for justice, mercy and peace is all in vain. Crassus delivers the final blow. With one swift deadly movement of his dagger, he slits the neck of the giant whose blood spatters his murderer's brow.

Spartacus is not to die, not yet. The memory of the black

giant will live on forever. His act of sacrifice will be immortalised. His name is Draba.

At the day's end, the dead body of Draba, is purposefully put on display to provide a salient lesson to the gladiators as to the fate of each one. The bleeding corpse hangs upside down in the central open space of the gladiators' dormitory.

As each one is made to file past, he is reminded of the merciless cruelty of Rome, of the pointlessness of resisting an indomitable force, and of the certain destiny of the vanquished. The intention is to make each gladiator desire to be a survivor, to aspire to be a victor whose success will be measured by his entertainment value in the arena.

To Spartacus the death of Draba is the death of a friend and the birth of a dream. The spirit of sacrifice will live on and endure. It will provide the flame that ignites the accumulating stockpile of combustible material turning it into an unquenchable blazing revolution that will end the Roman Empire.

DID HE HURT YOU?

She is very beautiful. Attention to her skin, so soft and porcelain white, is drawn by the perfect high cheekbones. Her hair is long, smooth and dark; her eyes, blue green in colour, appear to be on the edge of tears, indicating a cry for a former life in one so very young. She is British which does not itself explain her radiant beauty but perhaps does account for a defiant spirit towards an invading Roman army that has forced her into slavery. She is now the property of Batiatus. Her name is Varinia.

Crassus has noticed her and is considering buying her. Batiatus does not wish to sell but money makes an unignorable impression on everyone's thinking. Helena is content to let her husband spend a tiny fraction of his vast wealth on a new handmaiden. It allows her some room to pursue her interests in other men, a calculation based on an equation involving goose and gander.

One of the unusual pleasures that Batiatus has chosen to bestow upon his gladiators is the company of a woman on selected evenings. The bevy of female slaves line up to be assigned by Marcellus to the various cells where the gladiators sleep. Varinia is stood ready for her partner. Marcellus declares a name but his choice is usurped by Batiatus. Spartacus is to be her partner.

He waits, the door opens, she enters and moves past him standing against the wall with the window onto a closed world, and starts to disrobe. He is transfixed. He has never been with a woman before. He is so gentle in absorbing her beauty via the softest brushstrokes of the palm of one hand on her bare shoulder. He does not know where to go or how yet he yearns to explore this inexpressible beauty.

Two pairs of eyes glare down from the spyhole in the roof. The glee turns to disappointment. Now we know why Batiatus countermanded Marcellus. Spartacus is outraged. His owners have raped him. A moment of utmost privacy and intimacy has been grotesquely violated. He exclaims:

"I am not an animal"

The eyes disappear. Spartacus screams out his protest yet again. He turns to Varinia. He wants to apologise for them, for himself, for life itself. In an almost inaudible voice he repeats:

"I am not an animal"

"Neither am I"

It is the softest and strongest of replies.

Silence rightfully reigns over two people who began something that would never end that had no beginning but which gave both new life.

The door is thrown open. Batiatus enters and Marcellus seizes Varinia. Batiatus expresses his disappointment with Spartacus telling him:

"Tonight she will sleep with the Spaniard".

Spartacus is left alone, with his thoughts, and an indelible memory of Varinia.

Sometime later, the gladiators are seated in a line waiting to have their bowls filled by the passing female slaves serving the one meal of the day. Varinia is one server and Spartacus sits in his place contemplating how he might indicate to her his feelings. How do you, without words express a lifetime of emotions with a total stranger with whom you have determined to spend the rest of your days, with no prospect of freedom and little more probability of life itself?

For either to speak would cause the removal of the tongue offending and the guards watch carefully for any violations of the regime. She approaches, his mind races, he has chosen his four words that speak volumes of an undying love, of the deepest concern for her, of his defiance of the rulers of their world, one from which they will break free, knowing not how.

She fills his bowl. He looks into those nervous eyes.

"Did he hurt you?"

She is surprised, shocked even, but she also has confirmation of reciprocity. They are meant to be. She risks a whisper,

"No".

She intermittently looks back as she continues on her way. Spartacus looks to a new future.

Marcellus is not unaware of the exchange of glances between Spartacus and Varinia. When he learns that the woman has been sold to Crassus and is being taken at this very moment to Rome he seeks to goad Spartacus. It is a grave error, one that alters the future. On such grains of sand does the whole world turn.

The potential loss of Varinia is too much for Spartacus to bear. In a furious rage he wrestles with Marcellus forcing his head into an enormous bowl of stew and drowning him in the remains of the gladiators' meal. As other guards come to the aid of their beleaguered chief so also do other gladiators rally to their adopted leader. A mob quickly forms. There is no way back for the rebels now. It is do or die.

Batiatus is smart enough to know what the outcome will be, so he makes his escape abandoning his business, which within minutes has now become the gladiators' palace. It is the start of a rebel army which cannot be satisfied by taunting the Roman servants, treating them as a gladiatorial parody.

Spartacus addresses the crowd citing the memory of Draba as motivation for a new order. The rebel army will grow into a multitude, defeating undermanned opposition from cohorts of the Roman army, freeing slaves as they go thereby recruiting new freedom fighters, and finally escaping Italy.

She lives in his heart and he in hers. If only he can now find her.

I'M SPARTACUS

He was no soldier, but he knew how to fight. He was a magician and singer of songs, which are not obvious skill sets that an army needs. His tricks confused and amused. His songs made Spartacus dream of a better life, a different world. He had been the manservant of Crassus and managed to escape the compound while the household slept, drawn by the call of the growing slave army. That kind of resourcefulness would be valuable to the cause. Also, the slave army would need some special tricks to defeat their Roman adversaries. Inspiring songs would be helpful to achieve victory, to risk all for a life of freedom. So the young man is recruited. His name is Antoninus.

Varinia had escaped from Batiatus as he and his small entourage fled the gladiator school in Capua seeking refuge in Rome. On the way, she had insisted that she needed to go to the bathroom urgently and Batiatus was unable to cope with her constant protests. She had fled when he was not looking and seeing her disappear in the distance could not give flight being far too corpulent.

She had run and run and run, not knowing where she was fleeing, all the way into the arms of Spartacus. They consummated their reunion and Varinia became pregnant. Spartacus had become a rebel, a leader of men, a champion of the oppressed, a commander of a slave army, a husband and was now soon to be a father. There were no limits to this progression - save the person of Crassus.

The slave army fought a spirited campaign, but its members were not professionals. This multitude of farmers, artisans and servants, including old men and women and children feeding on their mothers' breasts, posed no match to the collective Roman armies of Italy, under the supreme command of Crassus.

The final bloody battle had to end with the slaughter of innocents. The battlefield was littered with corpses, many Roman soldiers but the vast majority those of slaves, freed to experience the afterlife.

A rump of fighters remains. These hundred or so men sit chained atop a mound listening to an offer made by a Roman herald:

"I bring a message from your master Marcus Licinius Crassus, commander of Italy. By command of His Most Merciful Excellency, your lives are to be spared. Slaves you were and slaves you remain. But the terrible penalty of crucifixion has been set-aside on the single condition that you identify the body, or the living person of the slave called Spartacus"

That's the choice then – live as a slave or die on the cross. The ticket to freedom and life is revealing the identity of your beloved leader, surrendering him to excruciating suffering and a slow death. Spartacus knows what he must do. He begins to rise to his feet but Antoninus is far too quick. He is on his feet declaring

"I'm Spartacus"

Spartacus looks at him dazed. Next comes Crixus, shouting

"I'm Spartacus"

Then there is David and next Dionysius. One after the other men rise to their feet shouting their new name, identifying themselves with their hero and inspiration. They shall not allow him to suffer the ignominy of hanging on a cross, not while they have breath in their bodies. He must live, and live forever that slavery may die.

A spontaneous chorus erupts from a choir of beaten men brought back to life by this perfidious gesture. Spartacus sits, the tears running down his cheek. Victory has been snatched from the jaws of defeat.

The road of crosses stretches endlessly to the horizon where it vanishes from sight. Every 50 metres a rebel hangs suspended between heaven and earth. The bodies of 6,000 crucified slaves line the Appian Way. Those dying can savour the memory of a final rebuke to the herald of Crassus. The dead are free at last. For dust they were and to dust shall they return save for the hope of a better life in eternity secured by a death on a cross in another place and another time.

It is night and a handful of men remain, including Spartacus and Antoninus. These residuals shall fight tomorrow in the temple of the ancestors of Crassus. It is to be one final spectacle to entertain the citizens of Rome and to reassure them that nothing can defeat her Imperialistic ambitions.

But Crassus is uneasy. He has recovered Varinia following the final battle and she has indicated that

Spartacus still lives. Crassus must know for himself. He searches among the survivors and finds Antoninus his former manservant. He is seated next to Spartacus. Crassus knows it is he. He insists that the two of them shall fight now, to the death, and the victor shall be crucified. He is determined to test to the limit this myth of the brotherhood among slaves.

A circle of Roman soldiers rapidly forms enclosing the former commander of the slave army and the singer of songs. They each have a sword. Their exchange is peerless:

"Don't give them the pleasure of a contest. Lower your guard, I'll kill you on the first rush."

"I won't let them crucify you!"

"It's my last order, obey it!"

"I won't"

"Do you realize how long it takes to die on a cross?"

"I don't care!"

Days ago, in response to the Roman herald, Antoninus was first on his feet to declare "I'm Spartacus". Nothing has changed. He will not let these barbarians crucify his leader. He would rather kill him, and be crucified as his substitute, but a singer of songs is no match for a skilled gladiator. No magic tricks will work for him now.

Antoninus draws blood at that first rush. It surprises Spartacus and yet it doesn't. Spartacus overpowers his young ward, pins him to the ground, already fatally wounded.

"I have loved you Spartacus as I loved my own father

And I have loved you as the son I shall never see. Go to sleep"

And with that final farewell, Spartacus ends the boy's life, trusting it is the start of a new one, a heavenly life that is endlessly free, entirely painless and filled with inexpressible joy. Spartacus turns to Crassus:

"Here's your victory. He'll come back. He'll come back, and he'll be millions!"

THE PICTURE'S PARABLE

The story of Spartacus and his campaign for freedom is wonderfully told in the 1960 film *Spartacus*. The making of that film exhibits many interesting features. Peter Ustinov, one of the film's stars was a brilliant raconteur as well as actor and writer. His tales of the film's journey to the screen, told from the other side of the camera, are particularly telling. I have drawn on these in setting a context for understanding the film's deeper messages.

Ustinov won the Best Supporting Oscar of 1961 for his fascinating portrayal of Batiatus. None other than Sir Laurence Olivier played the cruel Crassus, a nemesis for whom was Gracchus, an obdurate Roman senator brilliantly played by Charles Laughton. Ustinov had to befriend Laughton during the making of the picture to cater for his acute vulnerability and sensitivity which apparently was senselessly exploited by Olivier.

So needy did Laughton become that Ustinov was asked to script the scenes that involved these two alone together, when they discuss Varinia and Crassus towards the climax of the film.

A young and emerging Tony Curtis played Antoninus, a radiantly beautiful British actress, Jean Simmons, played Varinia, and the enigmatic Woody Strode played Draba.

Many other 'lesser' stars of the 50s and 60s adorned the cast making the ensemble almost as powerful as the Roman Empire itself, all of which contributed to its total Oscar haul of 4. It had been nominated for 6 Oscars though no leading categories such as Best Picture, Best Director or Best Actor were included in the 6.

Kirk Douglas, who of course played the eponymous hero, bossed the entire operation as executive producer. It was Mr Douglas who fired Tony Mann as Director and replaced him with Stanley Kubrick, with whom he had worked so enjoyably on *Paths of Glory* in 1957.

Dalton Trumbo, a severely blacklisted writer at the time of the McCarthy years, wrote the screenplay. The script was based on the book by Howard Fast. The entire production in many ways mirrors the underlying narrative that Spartacus projects, given that the film is more than mere entertainment.

Candidates for that deeper message might be taken as: the struggle for freedom, the striving for justice, the perils of imperialism, or the evils of prejudice.

When I think of the film as a story that Jesus may have told, I cannot get away from the centrality of sacrifice in the picture and its inspirational role in those inalienable values such as life, liberty and the pursuit of happiness.

I have concluded that the primary message of the film is that **sacrificial acts are contagious** and that sacrifice, far from being a defeatist move, is the secret for victory. I'd like to take some time now to explain why this is.

There are three prominent examples of sacrifice in the film that stand out as unmissable signposts to the parable. The first of these comes via the character of Draba.

This part calls for a ridiculously muscular and uniquely athletic person. Woody Strode who played the part was an athlete before he turned to acting. He was a top-notch decathlete and football star at UCLA before he turned to acting.

Even allowing for a resourceful and powerful figure such as Kirk Douglas, Spartacus was no match for Draba; it was far from being a battle of equals. The outcome was inevitable, and so it proved.

But Draba over-powering Spartacus and having him at his mercy was not the final outcome. It was but a stage in a process. Draba turns to Helena for permission to spare the life of his defeated opponent. Though Draba was clear favourite to win, the contest had been close. The two opponents had fought well; the crowd had been fully entertained. Although it could not be guaranteed, enough had been done to secure a merciful act, the sparing of the life of Spartacus. This, from a cynically materialistic viewpoint, would at least allow for a rematch that any entrepreneur would eagerly promote. Helena was not persuadable; she demanded death; according to her system of values, defeat deserved nothing less.

I wonder if Draba saw something in Spartacus that must be kept alive. He had sought friendship from a potential adversary when he had asked Draba for his name. Maybe Spartacus saw friendship as a bond that would be stronger than the desire to survive by killing others? Maybe Spartacus saw a different way to live, the way of friendship, of trust and of love?

Maybe Spartacus rejected the 'dog eat dog' lifestyle and valued instead a love thy neighbour approach, even if that neighbour is motivated to harm you? If Draba saw in Spartacus a better way to love, he concluded he saw a better way for him to die. And so he gave up his life that Spartacus, his new friend, might live. Of course there was as much chance of Draba harming the Roman crowds as there was of Spartacus beating him in the arena, which is next to none. Draba knew what he was doing; he was laying down his life in an unmistakable act of sacrifice.

The body of Draba was hung on public display as a warning to other gladiators. But to Spartacus it became an ineradicable reminder of that act of sacrifice, one that fuelled his dream of a better way to love. This gruesome display of a corpse backfired. Far from enervating the gladiators it energised them to new heights, to new acts of sacrifice that would in time bring freedom that could not be secured by waging war, but by pursuing peace.

The second act of sacrifice gives us the famous line from the film and the chorus from a perfunctory choir of defeated warriors, disintegrated by battle but unified in the pursuit of peace.

What exactly were Antoninus and all the other followers of Spartacus, saying in making the self-evidently false claim "*I'm Spartacus*"? Many things.

They were saying, 'Take me, for my life is better spent in reinforcing your belief that Spartacus is dead, that the idea that burned within him has been extinguished. Kill me and see how that idea is vivified in what they were saying.

"*I'm Spartacus*" further says that 'I have joined the cause that overcomes fear and a ferocity to fight my opponent with the faith that friendship can build bonds stronger than oak'.

"*I'm Spartacus*", in factual terms a false statement, is a true identification with the man whose name is Spartacus. It is saying to him, 'You are not alone, your belief in freedom for all is right and just, your practice to learn someone's name as a basis for a friendship that becomes a brotherhood is noble and good'.

The Romans are deaf to this and confused by the chorus. To them it is a cacophony that means all shall die, unaware that this idea can never die.

The final act of sacrifice that the film paints is the willingness of Antoninus to hang on the cross knowing his spiritual father will not have to suffer that curse.

This act reminds me of the time when Peter protested to Jesus that he will never allow the Jewish leaders to put him to death. That was so typical of Peter and to be fair to him he did cut off the ear of Malchus, the servant of the high priest, when the Jews were led by Judas to arrest Jesus in the garden of Gethsemane. What did Jesus do? He put the ear back; he told his disciples 'No swordplay', and he went to the cross.

He set his face like flint, knowing the cross to be his destiny, because he knew that no human being could suffer that death themselves; only he had the power to go through that pain and so defeat death.

As Spartacus hung on the cross, Varinia came to him bearing his son. She told her husband that his son was free, that she will tell him all about his father, that he will grow up free, proud and strong, and that she will teach him how to finish the work that his father had started.

I said there were three acts of sacrifice; each in their turn leading to a multiplication of sacrificial acts somehow invisibly orchestrated to achieve lasting peace. In fact, there is a fourth, and it is easily overlooked. It is at the very beginning of the film and is undertaken by none other than Spartacus.

When he bites the hamstring of the Roman guard who is beating the fallen slave, Spartacus surely knows full well that he is surrendering his life, and he does so in the hope that his fellow slave will be spared a beating and free to carry on living. We do not know what happens to the old man who fell by that wayside. We do know that before Spartacus finally dies, he brings life and hope and faith to many. His sacrificial act proves to be the genesis of many more.

When he says to Crassus: '*Here's your victory. He'll come back. He'll come back, and he'll be millions!*' Spartacus is perhaps without realising it, prophesying.

It is as if God the Father is speaking these words to the evil that temporarily rules this world, embodied in the person of Crassus. Here is their prophetic meaning.

Jesus hangs on the cross, breathes his last and gives up his spirit to his father in heaven. The earth shakes and some tombs are emptied. The dead within them walk the earth.

Jesus was killed, he did die and he was buried. He was in that virgin, borrowed tomb, sealed and guarded, for 3 days and nights. He was as dead as a doornail. But he rose from the dead, he ascended into heaven and he sent his Spirit to live in believers by their millions.

The victory of evil was not the death of Jesus but ironically the resurrection of all who are dead and to whom abundant life is now given.

He came back, and he is millions. That's why Spartacus is a great movie.

FREEDOM FROM DEATH

I was given a picture. Not like a painting in a frame, more of an idea. I don't know whether it was a dream or a vision. Maybe it just came to me while I was napping, I don't know. I'd probably been thinking a lot about that '*I'm Spartacus*' scene.

I often dwell for ages on just one scene from a film and then something occurs to me, dawns on me really, which I'd never got before; something that is really worth talking about. Anyway, this picture that I was given thrilled me and I thought I'd share it with you.

I am in a room with a lot of other people. I know some of them but many of them are strangers. There is no talking amongst the group, not even murmurings. It's as if everyone is waiting for something to happen but they don't exactly know what.

It's a cold, inhospitable room. The walls are bare, there is nothing about them to stare at, no relief. It is a waiting room where you wouldn't want to spend much time, but what might come next could be worse, so no one complains.

Questions appear on each face, 'Why am I here?' 'Who has done this to me?' and 'What comes next?' Nothing is vocalised. People sit on the floor in silence, just waiting but for what they have no idea. It's hard to find a common factor why this particular group is gathered. Is it a dentist's waiting room, or a doctor's surgery? Nobody knows. Time passes and silence remains.

A door opens and three men enter. Two of them are huge and strong, like Draba, except they are not black they are white. They wear uniforms that are black, and they have black ties that stand out against white shirts. They have shades, dark glasses, the kind that secret service agents wear - those guardians of the President of the US. The third man is smaller, his companions protect him but he is not the President. He looks more like a messenger from the President. Maybe that is who he is, but what have I got to do with the President? My questions grow but there are never answers. We, on the floor, are all in the same boat.

The small man starts to speak.

"You here, all of you seated in this room, have been found guilty and are now under the sentence of death. There is no right of appeal and the death sentence is to be carried out as soon as you are escorted from this room"

The small man looks at his large guardians. They make no movement. The shades give no clues as to whether their eyes blink. Murmurings among those seated begins softly, inaudibly, anxiously.

"I have here a list of names which I shall read out. When I call out your name, you must stand up and then you will be taken out of this room and put to death. When I have finished the list, all those who remain shall be free to go"

A wicked smile creeps across the small man's face. He has already said that all are guilty, that all are under the sentence of death, that there is no right of appeal. Why would someone's name not be on the list? He is teasing, teasing with death. He is offering false hope. Each must wait for their name to be called, somehow wishing, hoping, and praying that their name will not be called. But everyone knows that this man will call out the name of everyone sat on the floor. There is no hope. People wait for death.

The small man calls out the first name.

"Matthew!"

A guy gets to his feet and says,

"I'm Matthew"

The secret service guys go over to Matthew and escort him out of the room. We all watch, except for the small man. He is fixated on his list. The men in black re-enter and the small man calls out the second name on the list,

"Mark!"

A second guy struggles to his feet. He is elderly, not like Matthew who was young, about 33 I'd say. Mark looks much nearer death. He declares,

"I'm Mark"

When I look again he doesn't seem that old. Maybe the nearness of death has made him look younger. He's ready to go, he's prepared. The more I look, the more I realise that this second guy looks like exactly like Matthew, but it can't be him, because he's dead. The men in black take Mark out of the room and return without him. Who is next on the list?

"Luke"

I see a pattern here, but maybe it's pure coincidence. Matthew, Mark, Luke … I know what name comes next. I know the names of the four gospels, the first four books of the New Testament, in the Bible. As my mind races I notice a striking resemblance between the three of them. If I didn't know any better I'd say that all three of them were the same guy, but that can't be surely?

I wait for my name to be called. John is next, if the pattern is what I surmise. John is not called. The small guy reads out Peter, James, Andrew, .. a whole bunch of a names, but John is not on the list.

The room should be empty by now, except for me, but there are just as many seated on the floor as there were at the beginning. I must be dreaming. What is this picture?

The small guy says,

"I've come to the last name. John"

That's me. It is now my turn. I am guilty. I am to be put to death. There is no appeal. I look at the secret service guys. They do not flinch. I know what they are waiting for. I struggle to my feet. I'm not quick enough. This other guy stands up. He is much younger than me. He looks like

Matthew, and Mark and Luke. He is the same guy every time, for the first three plus Peter, James and Andrew. It's always the same guy. The secret service guys don't care. They have their job to do. Get the guy that stands up and march him out to his death.

This same guy has stood for each one of the people whose name has been called. Now he stands for me. I hear my substitute say,

"I am John".

He looks at me, and smiles. He does not wink. His smile is gone when he turns to the eyeless men in black. I do not speak. I make no protest. This is what this guy does. He's done it for everyone. I have no idea how he does it, my only clue as to why he has done it is his smile, his winning smile.

The secret service guys take 'John' out of the room. They do not come back. The small guy says,

"I have read all the names on the list. I am now finished. If you are still seated you are now free to go"

The small guy leaves, the door is left ajar. People struggle to their feet and start to leave and so do I.

As I reach the door, I put my hand on the arm of one of my floor mates. I had noticed that he had been sitting next to the guy who stood up for me. They had been talking while they waited for the small guy to get to the next name on the list. I want to know what they talked about. I ask,

"Hey mate, what do you make of that then? Was your name called? They called my name, but another person took my place. I saw him talking to you. I was wondering what you chatted about. Did you get his name?"

My floor mate nodded. He confirmed that they had been talking about many things. They spoke about guilt and innocence, punishment and reward, grace and mercy, redemption and renewal, sacrifice and love, life and death. They had spoken of all manner of such deep things. Then finally he said,

"His name is Jesus"

4 IT'S A WONDERFUL LIFE

ANSWER TO PRAYER

He is not really a praying man, but he's at the end of his rope and he doesn't know what else to do, where else he can turn. The bank examiner is in town and will surely find a deficit in the accounts of Bailey Building and Loan. The shortfall in income is easily explained but no-one will believe it, and everyone will think the worst.

George Bailey faces scandal, financial ruin and jail, and it's not his fault. Uncle Billy has misplaced the $8,000 he took to the bank to deposit but it's George who will pay the price. He is now quietly praying because he doesn't want anybody else to hear

'Dear Father in heaven, I'm not a praying man, but if you're up there and you can hear me .... please show me the way, I'm at the end of my rope, show me the way'.

George had stormed out of the family home leaving his wife and 4 kids confused, hurt and distraught. He asked Henry Potter for help but the owner of the bank, and nearly everything else in Bedford Falls, is in no mood to come to the aid of someone who has been a thorn in his side for years. This is Potter's chance to remove the final obstacle to his long-held ambition to dominate the town.

George sits at the counter of Mr Martini's bar sipping on a shot of rye to settle him down. He has helped Giuseppe Martini and his family to own his own home, along with countless other families now enjoying the delights of Bailey Park. These refugees from the rundown rentals owned by the oppressive Mr Potter is another reason why Potter hates George and wants him gone.

Martini wants to help the man who helped him but there's not much he can do. He knows drink is not the answer whatever the problem is.

"Why you drink so much my friend? Please go home Mr Bailey"

George waits to see if prayer is the answer, if his prayer will be answered, if God is concerned for his situation, if he is even listening.

"Bailey? Which Bailey?"

The query comes from the man sat next to George. It's Mr Welch. George doesn't know him, but then George didn't know his wife either when he spoke to her on the telephone about out an hour earlier concerning his poorly daughter Zuzu.

"This is Mr George Bailey"

Nick's identification is the trigger that Welch needs to swing a vicious right cross that busts George's lip, offering by way of explanation:

"Next time you talk to my wife like that, you'll get worse! She cried for an hour! It's not enough she teaches stupid children to read and write, you had to bawl her out"

Welch has outstayed his welcome and is marched out of the bar by Nick under Martini's orders. He'll not come back. Neither will George call on God again. He has the answer to his prayer. Nothing doing.

Clarence is a second-class angel. What this means inter alia is that he is yet to earn his wings. In order to do so he must prove his worth on some test or other. That opportunity has now appeared in the person of George - and much prayer.

After George quit the Bailey residence, understandably angry and distressed, his wife Mary called a few people to pray for George. Here are a few of those prayers offered on behalf of George, from friends and family:

I owe everything to George Bailey. Help him, dear Father. Emil Gower

Joseph, Jesus and Mary. Help my friend, Mr Bailey. Giuseppe Martini

He never thinks about himself, God, that's why he's in trouble. Bert the cop

George is a good guy. Give him a break, God. Ernie Bishop the cab driver

Help my son, George, tonight.

I love him, dear Lord. Watch over him tonight. Mary

Please, God, something's the matter with Daddy. Janie

Please bring Daddy back. Zuzu

Pretty impressive testimony wouldn't you say Clarence? You can tell something about a person by the prayers that people offer on their behalf when they need help from above. You'd expect prayers from your family but when your friends get on their knees you know it's for someone special.

When word gets out that someone is in trouble and it's

not their fault, that's when you get to know who your friends are and get to see the lengths they are prepared to go to in order to bring help.

Clarence is that help. He may only be second-class, but he's determined, and he's got God on his side.

THE RELUCTANT SAVIOUR

Every story that involves the heavenly realm has its own version of what that is like, for example in terms of admission policies and 'house rules'.

In some stories, like in the films *Ghost* and *The Sixth Sense*, the dead are not admitted until they get to finish a particular job on earth. In others, such as *The Bishop's wife* it is be about how angelic beings are sent to the aid of someone on earth in distress, a person in need of divine intervention.

In our story, heaven contains a vast library of videotapes of every person's every day spent on earth. Now that can be scary. Only I know what I've thought, said and done in secret and I'm pretty sure I would be embarrassed if the tapes of these private scenes were exhibited to others. In fact, being honest I'm ashamed of a great many things I've done.

But when Clarence is shown some of the tapes of George's life it is so he can get a better understanding of the person, as a young boy and as a man at various stages of life.

Heaven does not expect Clarence to be able to help George without him first knowing something about him. The test that Clarence is put through in order to win his wings is made that little bit easier by watching George grow up, listen to his ambitions, see how he behaves with other people and understand what his values are. We're going to take a peek over the shoulder of Clarence to see if we can see what he sees!

In the first scene, George is 12 years old and sledding with his friends on the snow and ice of a frozen river near their hometown of Bedford Falls. George's 9-year-old

76

brother Harry is careering down the riverbank where the surface is more slippery than normal. Harry skids out of control falling into the far distant icy waters of the river. George, without a moment's hesitation, plunges into the freezing waters to rescue his little brother but in the process develops an ear infection that leaves him permanently deaf in his left ear.

Harry however is saved and goes on to great success in life including becoming a decorated war hero as a fighter pilot in World War II. His daring deeds include defending hundreds of US sailors on board a vessel that was being attacked by Japanese bombers. All of these brave fighting men kept their lives because George saved Harry's life twenty-five years previously.

Clarence makes a note of George's heroics.

In another scene, George is working for Mr Emil Gower the local pharmacist in Bedford Falls. Part of his duties involves delivering prescription medication to Gower's customers. On one occasion Mr Gower receives a telegram informing him that his son has passed away having developed pneumonia during the Spanish flu epidemic of 1919.

Mr Gower is utterly distraught and makes a tragic error in dispensing a poison in the medicine for a customer. George is there to spot this mistake but cannot reason with Mr Gower who is completely inconsolable and incapable of recognising his error. George knows to ask his dad but his dad is too busy arguing with Henry Potter over how Bailey Building and Loan is going about its business.

George knows not to deliver the dangerous package and returns to the drug store with the poisonous medicine. Gower is on the telephone listening to the complaints of his customer who is yet to receive her medication. When Gower attacks George for his delinquency, that gives George a chance to explain to Mr Gower his reason for not delivering the medicine.

Gower is saved. Were it not for George, the woman complaining on the phone would have taken the wrong medicine and died. Emil Gower would have been found guilty of manslaughter and spent the rest of his life in jail.

It took discernment, determination and courage for George to make this intervention. He risked incurring the wrath of Gower, a beating and the loss of a job. It would make a dent in his reputation and the savings he was building up for his college education. But his action had saved a life. Clarence wonders how many lives has George saved – without the boy even realising it?

Life is filled with loads of invisible connections, which although they pass unseen by us do not go unnoticed by heaven above.

Clarence makes a further note. A clear picture forms in his mind.

Peter and Billy Bailey founded Bailey Building and Loan (BB&L) to help the citizens of Bedford Falls own their homes. The brothers believed that home ownership builds strong families and strong communities. While their company struggled continually in financial terms it demonstrated untold riches in its reputation for saving lives and strengthening ties among townsfolk.

BB&L was oxygen to the lungs of Bedford Falls.

George and Harry had personal ambitions that did not align with them remaining citizens of their town of origin. It is not unusual for small towns to provide a good grounding for its future generations and then let these 'fly the coop'. One way of looking at this diaspora of the young and ambitious is the planting of the town's values in other growing communities. Bedford Falls was a model example of community life, but ambition demands a bigger platform.

Peter Bailey understood this and was prepared for his sons to leave home and town, but not before they had served their time helping him run the company. He knew that his boys needed to graduate not only from school but also from the world of work. They could not otherwise fulfil their aspirations on the grander scale.

As Clarence continues to peruse the heavenly record, Harry is graduating from Bedford Falls High School and is about to take over from George as their father's assistant. George has deliberately delayed his own attendance at college in order to serve his time for his father at BB&L. Now it's Harry's turn – that was always the plan.

George has sacrificed 4 years of his life so that Harry can graduate from High School. Now Harry can hold the fort while George pursues his dreams of becoming an architect. All his life he has wanted to travel the world to see the great buildings that have inspired him to want to build airports, bridges, and skyscrapers. Bedford Falls is not big enough for George.

As George prepares to go to college, he gets news that his father Peter has had a fatal heart attack. The BB&L is under threat of extinction. One of its major shareholders is Henry Potter who amongst other things is owner of the town's bank and sworn enemy of Peter Bailey. Potter is calling for BB&L to fold.

George gives a spirited defence in the face of this vicious attack and impresses the board. The other shareholders vote to keep the business afloat – on one condition: that George takes the helm.

College is put on hold. Now this reluctant saviour is forced to make yet more sacrifices. It's Harry that goes to college while George keeps Bailey Building and Loan alive and in so doing helps fund new homes granting life to the poorer families. So many lives rescued, and George is not even keeping score.

But Clarence is reckoning that George is being schooled in sacrifice.

Mary Hatch has loved George for as long as she can remember. When she was 8 years of age she whispered into the deaf ear of her 12-year-old beau, '*George Bailey I will love you until the day I die*'.

Of course George didn't hear her and sadly he remained foolishly deaf to Mary's love until the day she graduated from college. Mary had never forgotten George and had remained faithful to him throughout her time at college. Now she was at home waiting for him to visit her.

An old friend of the pair, Sam Wainwright, calls with news of his booming business. Mary was happy for Sam's success, but she is not the least interested in money. George though is possibly envious of Sam's freedom to pursue his dreams while he is trapped in Bedford Falls.

Listening to Sam drone on means the couple must share the telephone handset bringing them cheek-to-cheek. George's sense of Mary's nearness dulls the sound of Sam's crowing and cajoling. Like magnetic poles that attract, George and Mary become inseparable, drawn into a world entirely of their own.

The scales fall from George's eyes and the symphony of Mary's love for her childhood sweetheart overcomes his deafness.

The couple leave Sam hanging on the phone while George sweeps Mary into his arms, the two enjoying a lengthy, tender embrace.

They are married within days and Clarence watches the happy couple climb into Ernie's cab to begin their honeymoon adventure.

Headed down Main Street Ernie notices hordes of people clamouring to get into the bank while a crowd gather at the prematurely locked doors of BB&L. This is a run on the bank, a mad scramble to extract cash before it's all gone. This is a financial crisis that George cannot ignore. The honeymoon must be put on hold.

It doesn't take long for George to recognise that Potter is behind this. It is the old man's desperate attempt to finally ruin BB&L. George has difficulty convincing the desperate crowd of savers who are demanding their money that there is no crisis. The problem is that George does not have enough cash.

But Mary does.

Like a triumphant warrior she holds aloft the great wad of cash that was intended for the honeymoon. Without thinking George takes the $2000 from the new Mrs Bailey seeing this as the means of victory over Potter.

When it comes time for the BB&L to close its doors at the legally appointed hour, two solitary dollar bills survive the stampede for cash. The honeymoon savings are all gone and with it the couple's adventurous beginning to married life. At least a dreadful misadventure has been avoided.

And it was a joint effort. George's life of sacrifice has infected Mary, and she could not be more delighted. She has her reward – the love of her life is her husband forever.

Clarence is now on a mission to keep things that way.

George and Mary have been married now for 14 years and they have four children – Pete, Janie, Tommy and Zuzu. Mary knows how to cut the family cloth according to its needs but life for the Bailey household is a daily struggle.

George has to live with the continual frustrations of never having been able to pursue his dream of becoming an architect. His life revolves around the same daily grind of the BB&L without making any progress. George is vulnerable and Potter knows it so the owner of the bank makes George an offer he cannot refuse.

Potter will give him a great job at the bank on ten times his present salary. George will be able to afford to take Mary on trips around the US and occasionally to Europe where they can take in the sights that George always wanted to see – the Eiffel tower, the Parthenon, and the Coliseum.

It is tempting but then the serpent in the Garden of Eden started all that malarkey.

George almost tastes of the fruit on offer but recognises that it is forbidden because it will mean the end of BB&L.

For most families in Bedford Falls the extinction of BB&L means the end of their dreams to escape from the horrible rentals that Potter provides and own their own homes.

George is not that kind of guy. Clarence can see that. George is instinctively a saviour of his fellow man though he would never identify with that description. That humility also is part of George's make-up. Sure he has dreams and ambitions but all of this is his way of improving the world for others to live in.

Clarence has done his homework on George and has a pretty good idea how to help him when the time comes.

George's heroics in saving Harry, in preventing the manslaughter of one of Gower's patients, in rescuing BB&L from extinction, in keeping BB&L afloat with the exhaustion of his honeymoon funds, and in refusing Potter's offer of a job all point to a life of contagious sacrifice. This is a life that is not self-seeking but one that serves the good of others, and the advancement of a community of souls.

The video vaults have served their purpose. Clarence now knows George better than George knows himself. The angel who is yet to graduate and gain his wings is ready to fly to the aid of this reluctant saviour, and very confident of helping him in his hour of need.

THE SECOND-CLASS SAVIOUR

It's Christmas Eve and that time of year when many people celebrate the birth of Jesus and give one another presents in recognition of God giving his son so that the world may not perish but have everlasting life.

George is planning to end his life and perish at his own hands. He rather hopes the hereafter into which he is about to pass will be better than the life he is ending, especially if it's going to last forever.

Uncle Billy has 'misplaced' $8,000 and suspicion will fall on George that he has been crooked with the money in BB&L. His last hope was Henry Potter who happens to have the $8,000. This was inadvertently handed to him by Uncle Billy folded up into the local newspaper bearing the headline 'Hero Harry Bailey returning home today'.

Potter of course refused to help George instead calling the police to arrest the alleged thief, ending his tenure with BB&L and thereby ensuring its demise. Bedford Falls now falls into the clutches of Potter.

At least the insurance money for George's death would take care of his family. George had figured that he was worth more dead than alive which explains why he is now about to miss Christmas day this year on account of throwing himself off the bridge and into the freezing waters of the river below.

Clarence has other ideas, thank God.

Two men stand on the bridge that overlooks the raging waters of the icy river below. One leaps in. The other sees the first man plunge into the dark, stirring waters below. He knows what he must do so in he follows struggling against the fast-flowing river and then against the first man who appears to be drowning. The rescuer is pulled safely to the side. Clarence has been saved. George has done what Clarence knew he would – he has rescued another life and unknowingly given himself the chance to be saved.

The two men dry out in the bridge tollhouse with the keeper looking on curiously. He grows even more bemused by these unexpected Christmas visitors as he eavesdrops on their conversation:

"So... you still think that killing yourself would make everyone feel happier, eh?"

"Oh, I don't know. I guess you're right. I suppose it would have been better if I'd never been born at all."

"What did you say?"

"I said I wished I was never born!"

"Oh, you mustn't say things like that... Oh, now wait a

minute. That's an idea now, isn't it?"

Clarence looks up to the ones that sent him.

"What do you think?"
"Ahhh... that will do it. All right, George... you've got your wish: you've never been born."

A violent gust of wind blows the door of the tollhouse open. It's God's sign. George has got what he wanted. It's also a lesson - be careful what you pray for.

Clarence tells George that he's got his wish granted, that he's never been born. George hears him clearly in his left ear – and why not? It was never damaged saving Harry when he was 12 because he's never been 12! Harry died in 1919. He never saved all those men on that ship. They all died. There is much about George's new life he has yet to discover, things that will horrify him.

George feels his lips. No blood. Mr Welch never struck him on the jaw because George didn't upset Mrs Welch. She doesn't teach George's kids – they don't exist. George is starting to get a little concerned. He wants to know who is this guy I rescued. He doesn't know it's his rescuer.

"Look, who are you? Who are you really?"
"I told you, George. I'm your guardian angel."
"Yeah, well what else are you? Are you a hypnotist?"
"No, of course not."
"Then why am I seeing all these strange things?"
"Don't you understand, George? It's because you were never born."
"Well, if I was never born... who am I?"
"You're nobody. You have no identity."
"What do you mean no identity? My name is George Bailey!"
"There is no George Bailey."

George searches his pockets for identification and finds none

"You have no papers, no cards, no driver's license, no 4F card, no insurance policy."

Clarence is starting to annoy George. He knows he took some rose petals from Zuzu when he was comforting her earlier that evening. He had secreted them in the watch pocket of his trousers. He searches for them. Of course, he can't find them. There is no Zuzu.

"They're not there either."
"What?"
"Zuzu's petals…"
"You've been given a great gift, George - A chance to see what the world would be like without you."

And so, the journey begins. Two men: one is an angel second class trying to get his wings, who had jumped into a river in order to save the other intent on committing suicide but who ends up being a rescuer instead; the other is a nobody who is really a very special somebody in the eyes of God, but he is yet to discover this truth.

George looks for his car but finds none. He enters what he thinks is Martini's but which is now Nick's and an altogether less salubrious place. The odd couple are thrown out, regarded as pixies for their bizarre conversation and George's embrace of Mr Gower, a felon recently released from a life sentence in jail for poisoning one of his patients.

Bedford Falls is Pottersville. Main street is littered with speak easies, bars, saloons, strip clubs, pay day loan shops each adorned by garish neon signs.

It should be called Horrorsville. Its citizens are addicted to drugs, alcohol, sex and gambling. They are slaves of Henry Potter without homes of their own, without families that stay together, existing but not living in the land of no hope.

It is a loveless hell. It is George's worst nightmare, but he has yet to see the worst when he discovers his own mother doesn't know him.

George looks at Clarence who says:
"Strange, isn't it? Each man's life touches so many other lives. When he isn't around he leaves an awful hole, doesn't he?"
"Clarence?"
"Yes, George?"
"Where's Mary? If this is all real and I was never born, what became of Mary?"
"Well... I don't... I can't..."

George grabs Clarence by the collar. He has to know.

"Look, I don't know how you know these things, but if you know where my wife is, you'll tell me.""
"I... I'm not supposed to tell."
"Please, Clarence, where's my wife? Tell me where my wife is."
"You're not going to like it, George."
"Where is she? What happened to her?"
"She became an old maid. She never married..."
"Where is she? WHERE IS SHE?"
"She's... she's just about to close up the library!"

George throws Clarence to the ground and runs off. He meets Mary as she locks up the library. She doesn't know this stranger. She's not his wife. She screams. Bert the cop arrives. He tries to arrest this maniac. George doesn't like to hit his friend but he has to. He has to escape. He has to get out of Pottersville. He has to get back to the bridge. He has to get back.

ANSWER TO PRAYER

He is not really a praying man, but he's at the end of his

rope and he doesn't know what else to do, where else he can turn.

He is back on the bridge. He is all alone. He isn't going to jump because there's no one to rescue, no one but him. So he prays:

Clarence! Clarence! Help me, Clarence! Get me back! Get me back, I don't care what happens to me! Get me back to my wife and kids! Help me Clarence, please! Please! I want to live again. I want to live again. Please, God, let me live again.

George is not asking for his old life back, he is asking for a new birth. He wants to get back to the life he once had but didn't really value. Now that he knows the value of the life he was foolishly going to end he can return a new person. He doesn't care about scandal, ruin and jail. He wants to be with his wife and kids. He values them more than any $8,000.

He is asking for a new life with the wife he loves, with the kids he loves, with the people he loves – even Mr Potter. George has learned who he is because of what God has made him.

God always hears prayer. He is always listening. He always answers. He knows what is best for us and always gives us that best.

It starts to snow. George's lip is bleeding. Zuzu's petals are in his watch pocket. Bedford Falls is restored. His kids are home. His wife is at the head of a train of friends that are flooding their house. The people of Bedford Falls have dug into their savings. They have collected more than the $8,000 – much more. Sam Wainwright has wired $25,000.

George is rich beyond his wildest dreams. He holds Zuzu in his arms with Mary by his side and the house is filled with joy, festooned with people whose lives have been rescued by George, saved from Pottersville.

A tiny bell perched on the Christmas tree rings. Zuzu

chimes up:

"Look, Daddy. Teacher says, every time a bell rings an angel gets his wings."

"That's right, that's right."

"Attaboy, Clarence."

Harry arrives having flown through a blizzard. The war hero toasts his big brother, the peace hero – 'The richest man in town'.

Inscribed in his copy of *'The adventures of Tom Sawyer'*, Clarence has left George a message:

Dear George:
Remember no man is a failure who has friends.
P.S. Thanks for the wings! Love, Clarence.

There's nothing second-class about God's work.

THE PICTURE'S PARABLE

This heart-warming story of George and those he touches is beautifully told in the film *It's a wonderful life* (1946). The part of George is played by James Stewart and many other stars join the cast, most notably: Donna Reed (Mary), Thomas Mitchell (Uncle Billy), Lionel Barrymore (Potter), and Henry Travers (Clarence).

The film was nominated for 5 Oscars including best picture, best actor, and best director. It won none. Jimmy Stewart thinks this is because just after World War II the audience didn't want that kind of movie, preferring war movies or slapstick (Red Skelton style).

The film was up against *The best years of our lives* which won 7 Oscars. But today few people remember that film whereas *It's a wonderful life* is shown every Christmas on TV to audiences all over the world, such is its lasting appeal and remarkable longevity.

It is Jimmy Stewart's favourite film of the 100 plus films

he made. We get a glimpse into his reasons for this by referring to his letter to the story's author Philip Van Doren Stern, dated December 31, 1946:

More important than anything, thank you for giving us that idea, which I think is the best one anyone has had for a long time. It was an inspiration for everyone concerned with the picture to work in it, because everyone seemed to feel that the fundamental story was so sound and right, and that story was yours, and you should be justly proud of it.

Why was the story 'so sound and right'? That's what I ask myself as I think about what it is that puts the film near the top of my list of favourites. Certainly, it is the special *moments* like when George is in Mr Martini's bar and he prays. He expresses simply but profoundly his deepest need – to know what to do, to know what is the way. There are many such *moments* and the film like any classic film captures these special *moments* that artists aspire for but must often wait for with extraordinary patience but with heightened expectancy.

In my search for knowing what this film, this story and these characters are all about I have concluded that the story is a parable which has an important truth to tell us and it is this – **prayer is the sacrifice we make in life to discover God's very best for our lives**.

I want to spend the rest of this chapter explaining this truth, by revisiting the story with new eyes and an open mind.

The central character in the story is unmistakably George Bailey and it turns out that he is the hub of a network of many characters including Mary, Billy, Potter, Bert and Ernie. Being a hub is a big responsibility. How does George bear this weighty load? Is he an influence for good or bad?

When we look at his life, we see a pattern that points to a sacrificial life, which is partially obscured by a driving ambition to abandon Bedford Falls and become an architect on a grand scale erecting skyscrapers, bridges and airports. George wants to make his mark and superficially this contradicts a life of sacrifice. Interestingly Jesus made his mark – he has many followers today – by being the ultimate sacrifice.

What does George have in common with Jesus? Very little it seems. He is not a praying man – Jesus prayed all the time. He is not content to spend his life in Bedford Falls – Jesus travelled relatively little. He got very angry when it appeared he would take the blame for something he didn't do – Jesus was accepting of carrying the can for others' mistakes. (It says somewhere – he was led like a lamb to the slaughter, yet he did not open his mouth). Have I got it wrong then in comparing George to Jesus? Where exactly is this evidence of a life of sacrifice?

In our story the prominent events that characterise the life of George are: rescuing Harry by risking his own life; saving the life of Mr Gower's patient by risking a beating, loss of income, and his reputation; allowing Harry to go to college by foregoing his own education in order to save BB&L; rescuing BB&L from bankruptcy by exhausting his honeymoon fund; preserving BB&L by resisting a tempting job offer from Potter; and, rescuing Clarence by risking his own life.

Now you may call him a reluctant saviour or an instinctive rescuer. You can minimise these events and marginalise George's efforts. Or you can see that it is part of George's nature to put others before self.

Of course, he is not perfect. He resents being cooped up in Bedford Falls and living a humdrum life that simply follows, trudges in fact, in his father's footsteps. This does not align with his dreams to become a great architect building landmarks for the world to admire and put to use in improving the quality of millions of lives. Would it not also be human nature to have such aspirations and to become bitterly frustrated when they are overturned by this instinct to neglect self in favour of others?

But let us look again at what George wanted to do and compare that to what he actually did. For if we do this, we shall clearly see a life of sacrifice and the comparison with Jesus is not that farfetched.

What is a skyscraper? At one level it is simply a tall building. Functionally, it is a way of maximising occupancy whilst minimising footprint. Aesthetically it is an indicator of the glory of architecture. Metaphorically it is a symbol of the power of the architect lending itself to expansive, over-the-horizon views, pointing to how visionary its conceiver is.

George Bailey built no ordinary skyscraper. His conception, made a reality through hard work, tenacity, endurance and belief, was Bailey Park. This development reached new heights for its occupants. It maximised their opportunity to build new lives for themselves whilst minimising their expenditure, which afforded them the opportunity to escape the slum tenements of Henry Potter and his financial grip on their lives.

Bailey Park is an indicator of the glory of community built not with concrete, steel and glass but the more precious materials of flesh, blood, bone and human spirit.

George Bailey was an architect – he just never knew it, until he prayed 'show me the way' and got Clarence as his guide. He came to realise that his life mattered and so he prayed again, '*Get me back. I want to live again. Please, God, let me live again.*' George came to know the meaning of his architecture and saw the great landmarks he had built when he witnessed the overwhelming love of his family and friends.

What is a bridge? In its simplest terms it is a structure that overcomes an obstacle, perhaps a river or a canyon, in order to bring two separate pieces of land together. Functionally, it is a means of supporting transportation and communication. The bridge that George built was Bailey Building and Loan. It was this invention, fashioned through sacrifice and determination, which enabled impoverished families to cross over from slavery to a cruel landlord to a new land of opportunity.

What is an airport? Viewed simplistically, it is a place where airplanes take-off and land. But if these aircraft carry neither cargo nor passengers what is the point? The airport that George built was Bailey Park. It was a launch pad for new beginnings, a take-off point for families to grow in strength of mind and body. It is place where community is mature and individuals take responsibility themselves and their fellow man. It is a landing point for others to be attracted to, where business can make investments bringing economic growth.

George wanted to be an architect and that is what God wanted for George. He just had different building materials and constructions in mind. And when George saw his life through the new eyes God gave him, he was glad he prayed.

It is worth noting that Jesus got to the end of his rope and what did he do? He prayed. This was in the garden of Gethsemane, an event recorded in the gospels and beautifully rendered in the song by Tim Rice and Andrew Lloyd Webber. He saw the way ahead as being hard and wanted to know if there was any other way. But he did not insist on his way, he accepted God's way.

On the cross Jesus asked 'God why have you forsaken me?' but prayed finally 'Father, into your hands I commit my spirit'.

George's suffering was unfair, and given the sacrifices he had made through his life it was especially unjust. But when he prayed he undertook the greatest sacrifice he could make.

Prayer admits that the situation is beyond your control, that you are handing over control to someone you can trust, someone you hope has the power to do something about it and has your best interests at heart. That is the meaning of prayer. That was George's ultimate sacrifice.

UNBELIEF, DOUBT AND PRAYER

He wasn't much of a praying man but that didn't stop him praying. It's interesting to take a look at George's two prayers because they reveal the progress he makes from desperation to supplication.

We don't know what George's prayer life was like after he got his new birth, but I am willing to bet that he prayed more because he got to know much more about who he was praying to, what he is like, and how the two of them could get along just fine.

George's first prayer went like this:

'Dear Father in heaven, I'm not a praying man, but if you're up there and you can hear me …. please show me the way, I'm at the end of my rope, show me the way'.

Think about what George is saying here. He knows that there is someone in heaven who people refer to as 'Father'. George would have been taught this at home and in school that this is the way to pray, so George like the rule-observing, well-behaved, conforming person that he is would follow suit.

But George confesses that he is unsure that this Father is 'up there' and that he 'can hear' him. This is typical of someone who is 'not a praying man' – and that's ok.

There are plenty of people who simply do not believe such a person exists, and that's ok. These folks are entitled to their unbelief and I have to say that the way many believers behave actually reinforce that unbelief, which is sad if not tragic.

But prayer is a journey and it can only start by leaving the station of unbelief. Once you're prepared to abandon the certainty that there is no 'Father in heaven', it does not matter one jot how much you doubt the existence of this person, the journey has begun. George begins his journey with the word 'if'.

Many people who dare to pray do so riddled with doubt that there is someone 'up there', that this someone can hear, that they will listen, especially to them, enmeshed in doubt as they are and completely confused about what they are attempting.

It's ok to doubt. I would even say it is healthy to doubt as long as you press on. That's what George did. He dared to ask for help.

OK, he thought the answer to his prayer was a sock on the jaw. Many people get confused about answers to prayer and that's ok.

From my perspective, God is 'up there', he can hear, he does listen, and he always answers. In my experience he's good at waiting, excellent at remembering and flawless in answering.

I have my doubts whenever I pray but I do know this for certain - God has my very best interests at heart and his answers to my prayer are always aligned with those best interests. Of that I have no doubt.

George's second prayer went like this:

Clarence! Clarence! Help me, Clarence! Get me back! Get me back, I don't care what happens to me! Get me back to my wife and kids! Help me Clarence, please! Please! I want to live again. I want to live again. Please, God, let me live again.

The tone has changed. George knows whom he is talking to – to Clarence and to the one who sent him – God. He knows this for certain. The station of unbelief is long gone, but he still has doubts because although he knows someone hears and someone listens, he cannot be sure how they will answer.

George puts no constrains on the answer. He does not '*care what happens*', he only wants to get back. He wants to see his wife and kids – even if that means them visiting him in jail! He does not want to die a living death in Pottersville; he wants to live again with new eyes, a new heart, and a new belief.

I think it's a great prayer. George might consider himself to be not much of a praying man but for me his prayers are as good as it gets. As not much of a praying man, whatever it is that George can look forward to, I for one bet *it's a wonderful life*.

5 THE SHAWSHANK REDEMPTION

There is a time for everything, and a season for
every activity under the heavens ...'

TIME TO KILL
'There is a time to kill and there's a time to heal'

He had high hopes always. A dutiful scholar he passed all his school examinations. At college he brooked no distractions, graduating cum laude. A job in the bank was guaranteed, the first rung on climbing the ladder. Now he was Vice President. In a very real sense he held people's lives in their hands. He could offer them hope by approving their home loan, or he could inflict despair by foreclosing on their mortgage. He made wise decisions. His power might have been the reason she was attracted to him.

She was beautiful and he was attractive to her. Though he was not that handsome, neither was he ugly. He had a powerful job and that stimulated her appetites. He had money and credit. His job, totally secure and very well rewarded, made borrowing a breeze should that be necessary. He was smart enough to know if and when. His future was bright. Then it wasn't.

He suspected she had been playing around. Maybe it was

the fact that he had put so many hours in at the bank, for her as much as for him. She found herself too often at a loose end. Maybe he had become too predictable, less interesting, in fact boring. Accountancy people can easily be stereotyped as boring. Rules and regulations guys are so predictable. She would get her fun playing around with the local golf pro whose swing had greater appeal.

When he confronted her the night before about her infidelity, she told her husband that she was glad that he had finally found out. She hated all the sneaking around. She wanted a quickie divorce in Reno. The marriage had died. Let's bury it for goodness sake.

He still had hopes, even as the bourbon blurred his razor-sharp mind. Threatening her and her lover would work. It would put the golfer out of bounds. It would bring her to her senses. She wouldn't fool around anymore once she could see how tough he could be, how tough although so marvellously gentle, how uncompromising and yet so very merciful, how rebuking but imperturbably conciliatory.

Why should he kill her when he loved her? He blames himself for her errant behaviour. He had not shown her the love he truly felt. He had driven her into the arms of this adulterous golfer. He had no need for a different wife. He was content with this one. When she saw his true love she would be his again.

He tossed the empty bottle of Kentucky's finest onto the floor of the sedan, sweeping it aside with his foot. He nursed the revolver. As he opened the car door, The Ink Spots came over the radio, serenading him with 'If I didn't care'. That's the point. He did care. He had hopes.

TIME TO EMBRACE
'There is a time to embrace someone and there's a time not to embrace'

Andy turned over recent memories in studied silence as he sat among the rest of the prisoners on the bus that carried them to Shawshank prison.

He had heard the verdict unmistakably. The twelve jurors were unanimous – 'Guilty' on both counts of first-degree murder. In a state of utter disbelief, he heard the sentence being pronounced – double homicide, life imprisonment, twice over, back to back.

His accountancy skills were not unduly exercised in reckoning he would die in jail, punished for crimes for which he protested his innocence.

The bus pulls to a standstill and the new fish as they are known file out in a line and form a parade for the benefit of the watching inmates who make bets, in the currency of cigarettes, on which of them will crack first. Red has two packs on Andy. Heywood prefers the fat one. It's a game played with every catch of new fish, with the winner making off with the pot of tobacco.

The Warden, Samuel Norton, inspects the line. He is an austere, self-righteous man, uncompromising in his discipline. He is the master of all he surveys, governing ruthlessly with the muscle of Captain Byron Hadley.

"I believe in two things: discipline and the Bible. Here you'll receive both. Put your trust in the Lord; you belong to me. Welcome to Shawshank"

On that first night the inmates go fishing, baiting the newcomers with thinly veiled taunts if not actual naked threats of sexual abuse and beatings. It's an initiation that makes it difficult for even the toughest to endure. Who is going to bite first? The taunt from Heywood to his chosen fish sends the fat one over the edge and lands him his prize.

Heywood's jubilation is short lived as he watches the monstrous Hadley indulge his insatiable sadism. Like a kind of demonic dervish, he wields his truncheon and beats the fat one to a pulp. The punishment concludes with a kick to the head. The fat one lies motionless on the prison block floor. All the fish fall silent. The lifeless body is hauled off to the infirmary. The doctor had gone home for the night so the fat one lies in his bed unattended and bleeding. When morning comes it's too late for anyone to do anything. This new fish hasn't made it. Shawshank suffers another loss, and Heywood has his winnings.

Andy has surprised Red. It won't be the last time.

Hope is not lost.

TIME TO GATHER
'There is a time to scatter stones and there's a time to gather them'

Ellis Boyd Redding, known to all as simply 'Red', has been in Shawshank for more than twenty years by the time Andy arrives. As a stupid kid in his late teens he foolishly committed one terrible crime. Red is now a veteran of multiple parole rejections, and elder statesman among Shawshank inmates. He is a cynical conformist, submissive to the system and suspicious of its members. He is both resigned and undefeated, a passionate exponent of the dangers of hope.

Red has learned how to get things for people. He is the uncrowned king of the invisible black market with his secret network of transfer agents. He is the unseen hub of furtive trade with an enviable stash of tobacco and cash, the booty of his canny deals.

That first night, Red had figured Andy to be a sure-fire quitter. He could not have been more wrong and his error of judgment cost him two packs of cigarettes. Andy never made a sound. It was the genesis of a growing admiration for Andy's resilience, focus, and determination, so when Andy came to him Red was prepared to help.

"I understand you're a man who knows how to get things. "

"I'm known to locate certain things from time to time."

"I wonder if you might get me a rock hammer?"

"What is it? And why?"

"A rock hammer is about six inches long - looks like a miniature Pickaxe."

"Pickaxe?"

"For rocks. I'm from a rock hound at least I was in my old life I'd like to be again on a limited basis."

"Or maybe you'd like to sink yours into somebody's skull."

"No I have no enemies here."

"No? Wait a while word gets around full queers take by force that's all they want or understand if I were you I'd grow eyes in the back of my head."

"Thanks for the advice."

"That's free - you understand my concern?"

"If there's any trouble, I won't use the rock hammer."

"I guess you'd want to escape? Tunnel under the wall."

Andy starts to laugh ...

"Did I miss something? What's so funny?"

"You'll understand when you see the rock hammer."

"What's an item like this usually go for?"

"Seven dollars in any rock and gem shop."

"My normal marker is 20% but this is a specialty item, risk goes up price goes up, let's make it an even ten bucks."

"Ten it is."

"Waste of money if you ask me."

"Why's that?"

"Folks around this joint love surprise inspections; if they find it you're going to lose it, if they do catch you with it you don't know me, if you mention my name we never do business again not for a shoe lace or a stick of gum - you got that?"

"I understand. Thank you Mr ...?"

"Red. "My name's Red."

In the spring of 1949, the powers that be decided that

the roof of the license-plate factory needed resurfacing. A group of 12 volunteers were needed for a week's work. May in the State of Maine is a fine time to be working outdoors. With Red's organisational skills and sphere of influence it was simple enough for his gang, which now included Andy, to be part of the detail.

As the work proceeds Andy happens to overhear a conversation Hadley is having with his men. He is complaining that a small inheritance he will receive from his brother-in-law, $35,000 will have a large chunk taken out by the IRS.

Red is concerned that Andy has stopped work to listen to the guards and that when they see that, it won't be good for Andy. Sure enough Hadley turns round and gives Andy an evil stare, the preface to a certain beating. Things only get worse when Andy asks if Hadley trusts his wife. Before Hadley throws Andy off the roof, he manages to force out a word of explanation:

"Because if you do trust her, there's no reason you can't keep that $35,000!"
"What did you say?"
"$35,000."
"$35,000?"
"All of it."
"All of it?"
"Every penny."
"You better start making sense."
"If you want to keep all of that money, give it to your wife. The IRS allows a one-time-only gift to your spouse for up to $60,000"
"Tax-free?"
"IRS can't touch one cent."
"You're that smart banker, who killed his wife, aren't you? Why should I believe a smart banker like you? So I can end up in here with you?"
"It's perfectly legal; go ask the IRS, they'll say the same

thing. I actually feel stupid telling you this, I'm sure you would've investigated the matter yourself. I suppose I could set it up for you. That would save you some money. If you get the forms I'll prepare them for you, nearly free of charge. I'd only ask three beers apiece for each of my co-workers. I think a man working outdoors feels more like a man if he can have a bottle of suds. That's only my opinion, sir."

It's not possible to say that Andy made a friend of Hadley that day – who befriends the devil? But things did change. Hadley was smart enough to make use of Andy and to see that he came to no harm other than what only he had the right to inflict upon him. Moreover, Hadley kept to the bargain and made sure the detail had their cold bottles of beer to enjoy in a rest break on the roof while enjoying the spring sunshine of Maine.

Heywood ambles over and offers Andy a 'cold one'. He politely declines and explains that he has quit drinking. He is simply content to see his friends having a good time and giving them an opportunity to remember what it is to be normal. That is Andy's reward.

An enigmatic smile creeps over his sun-kissed face. He has found a new use for the rock hammer. It will take time, but time is what he has in plenty. He might as well occupy it with wise investments just as any smart banker would. He has high hopes again.

TIME TO MEND
'There is a time to tear and there's a time to mend'

Bogs Diamond took a shine to Andy on the first day he arrived. This veteran convict led his own gang known as 'The sisters'. The innocent moniker was a disingenuous cover for who they actually were – ruthless rapists who preyed upon and beat their targets into submission performing unspeakable acts of sexual abuse upon their victims; acts that scarred their body and stripped them of their humanity.

Time and again The Sisters preyed upon Andy. Time and again he fell foul of Bogs, returning to his cell with fresh bruises, feeling slightly less human than before, being drained of hope.

The Sisters kept at him – sometimes he was able to fight them off, sometimes not. And that's how it went for Andy – that was his routine.

The first two years were the worst for him, and if things had gone on that way, Shawshank would have got the best of him, but amazingly relief came in the most unlikely person of Captain Byron Hadley. When Hadley discovered that Andy was in the infirmary and that Bogs had beaten him almost to death for blankly refusing to cooperate, he acted swiftly, decisively and mercilessly.

Bogs returned to his cell from a spell in solitary and Hadley was waiting there for him. The guards behind Bogs had been apprised. They were there not only to escort Bogs safely to his cell but also to ensure he could not escape the beating he would get from Hadley.

Two things never happened again after that. The Sisters never laid a finger on Andy again and Bogs never walked again. They transferred him to a minimum-security hospital upstate. As far as anybody knew, he lived out the rest of his days drinking food through a straw.

Hadley had executed a perverse act of justice on behalf of the fish that saved his taxes.

Free of the menace of the Sisters, Andy was able to concentrate on his new roles. Word had got out that the smart banker knew how to minimise tax liability and pretty soon guards were filing up outside a small office that Andy was given in the library where he now worked as an assistant.

Brooks was the man who pushed his cart around the prison cells dispensing books (and occasional items of contraband) for postprandial digestion. Brooks was Red's mule and fitted to the task exactly. He had been in Shawshank for 45 years, was as mild as a dove, incapable of insurrection, and completely believable as a librarian. Andy was better than a drug pusher. He was a legal and financial consultant par excellence.

Andy was a great help to the guards who could not help but appreciate him. The manner in which he befriended his keepers turned them from guards to guardians – a truly amazing metamorphosis.

Andy also made Norton an incredibly wealthy man, a secret to which he alludes in a private conversation with Red:

"Warden's got his fingers in a lot of pies, from what I hear."

"What you hear isn't half of it. He's got scams you haven't even dreamed of. Kickbacks on his kickbacks. A river of dirty money runs through this place."

"Yeah, but the problem with having all that money is sooner or later, you're gonna have to explain where it came from."

"That's where I come in. I channel it, filter it, funnel it: stocks, securities, tax-free municipals. I send that money into the real world and when it comes back its clean as a whistle. Cleaner. By the time Norton retires, I'll have made him a millionaire."

"Ever bother you?"

"I don't run the scams Red, I just process the profits. It's a fine line, maybe, but I also built that library and used it to help a dozen guys get their high school diploma. Why do you think the warden lets me do all that?"

"To keep you happy and doing the laundry; money instead of sheets!"

"If they ever try to trace any of those accounts, they're gonna end up chasing a figment of my imagination."

"Well, I'll be darned. Did I say you were good? You're a Rembrandt!"

"Yeah. The funny thing is - on the outside, I was an honest man, straight as an arrow. I had to come to prison to be a crook."

Andy could live with a clear conscience because he knew that the special treatment he received benefited all of the inmates. This was one of Andy's greatest hopes – that his time at Shawshank would edify the lives of all with whom he came into contact.

The development of the library was a big part of this mission. He implored the state government for funds by writing letters. Naturally they ignored him, but as he persisted they could not continue to brush this irritant under the carpet. After 6 years, they sent him a cheque for $200 and told him to stop writing his letters. He promised himself 'from now on, I'll write two letters a week instead of one'. And he did.

In 1959 the state senate finally clued in to the fact they couldn't buy him off with just a $200 check. Appropriations committee voted an annual payment of five hundred dollars just to shut him up. And you'd be amazed how far Andy could stretch it.

The library's augmented inventory included music recordings on vinyl platters. A fresh delivery arrives one day at the warden's office and Andy is ordered to get it to the library before the warden returns.

As he browses the package of books and vinyl he comes across the 'Duettino Sull'Aria from Le Nozze di Figaro. He loves this piece. He knows it would amaze his fellow inmates. Hearing it would be uniquely uplifting should they ever get the chance.

Andy notices that he has been left alone, his friendly guard is taking a bathroom break, so he locks the door of the warden's office, goes over to the record player, places the vinyl platter on the deck, and connects the output to the PA system.

This system is the exclusive property of the warden. It is

only ever used for the express purpose of addressing the prisoners on urgent items of the utmost importance. Andy reasons that nothing was more important or more urgent at that moment than to play this Mozart piece.

The cells are alive with the sound of music. The entire prison population, guards and cons, is brought to a complete standstill.

Amazement is not a big enough word to describe the looks on the faces of every single prisoner and guard. It cost Andy a month in solitary confinement. Its value was inestimable. Here's how Red summarises the experience:

"I have no idea to this day what those two Italian ladies were singing about. Truth is, I don't want to know. Some things are best left unsaid. I'd like to think they were singing about something so beautiful, it can't be expressed in words, and makes your heart ache because of it.

I tell you, those voices soared even higher and farther than anyone in a grey place dares to dream. It was like some beautiful bird flapped into our drab little cage and made those walls dissolve away, and for the briefest of moments, every last man in Shawshank felt free."

Where there is hope, there is freedom, and hope is contagious.

TIME TO SPEAK
'There is a time to be silent and there's a time to speak.'

Andy has parked his car a little out of sight from the house of the golf pro with whom his wife is having an affair. It has taken elementary detective skills to track the two of them down.

As he swigs on his bottle of bourbon, he envisages the choreography of entering the property and disturbing the couple who are probably in bed, either asleep after having had riotous sex or about to reach a climax.

He imagines warning the golf pro to lay off his wife, watching the coward collect his clothes together and make a hurried exit. He can see himself remonstrating with his wife and then telling her he forgives her, that he loves her, that things will be different.

What he does not know is they are already dead.

Tommy Williams arrived at Shawshank in 1965 on a 2-year sentence for breaking and entering having been caught stealing TV sets from JC Penney. He has a wife and baby daughter. He has spent times in prison since he was 13 years of age, including a spell in Thomaston, where he roomed with Elmo Blatch an habitual criminal, overbearing braggart and obsessed egomaniac.

Andy has spent the best part of 20 years tutoring fellow inmates so that they can get their GED, a qualification that will help them get rehabilitated and engaged in successful employment on the other side.

Andy is adding value in the lives of fellow human beings, investing in the release of the vulnerable.

He has few rules, but one is he won't waste his time with losers. Tommy wants to be one of Andy's tutees and shows that he is committed, so Andy takes Tommy under his wing, teaching him how to read.

A year later Tommy is ready to take the test but he gets frustrated and gives up before completing the test. Andy submits it anyway and when the result comes back Tommy has passed, obtaining a C+. He knows he could have done better if he'd stayed the course. He tells Red that he feels he has let Andy down.

Red reassures the kid that isn't the case, that Andy is proud of him and the two cons get to talking about their mutual friend. As Tommy listens to Red's story of Andy he realises that his tutor is innocent and explains why to Red:

"I was in a cell with this guy one time, the kind of roomie you pray you don't get, you know what I'm saying? He was doing 6 to 12 for armed burglary. He'd talk ALL the time; he'd never shut up. He said he pulled hundreds of jobs, so one night like a joke, I say to him, 'Yeah, Elmo? Who'd you kill?' So he says...

'I got me this job one-time bussing tables at a country club, so I could case all these big rich folk that come in. So, I pick out this guy, go in one night and do his place. He wakes up. So, I killed him. Him and this tasty lady he was with. That's the best part. She's in bed with this guy, this golf pro, but she's married to some other guy, some hotshot banker, and he's the one they pinned it on.'"

A prolonged period of stunned, respectful silence reigns over Red and Tommy as the horror of the situation gradually dawns on Red. Andy is told. The former banker turned chess set maker has no thoughts of remorse or regret. He only has his eyes set on a bright future, which is what hope always sees. He knows he can talk to the warden about this and get him to do the decent thing - secure Andy's release:

"I have to say that's the most amazing story I've ever heard. What amazes me most is that you were taken in by it."

"Sir?"

"Well, it's obvious this fellow Williams is impressed with you. He hears your tale of woe and quite naturally, wants to cheer you up. He's young, not terribly bright. It's not surprising he wouldn't know what a state he put you in."

"Sir, he's telling the truth."

"Well, let's say for the moment this Blatch does exist. You think he'd just fall to his knees and cry 'Yes, I did it, I confess! Oh, and by the way, add a life term to my sentence.'"

"You know that wouldn't matter. With Tommy's testimony I can get a new trial."

"That's assuming Blatch is still there. Chances are

excellent he'd be released by now."

"Well they'd have his last known address, names of relatives. It's a chance, isn't there?"

Norton shakes his head

"How can you be so obtuse?"
"What? What did you call me?"
"Obtuse. Is it deliberate?"
"Son, you're forgetting yourself."
"The country club will have his old timecards - records, W-2s with his name on them."
"If you want to indulge in this fantasy, that's your business. Don't make it mine. This meeting is over."

Andy spent a month in solitary for insubordination. When he came out he was given the news that Tommy was dead. Hadley shot him trying to escape.

In fact Tommy was murdered. When the warden interviewed Tommy he affirmed that he would testify under oath that his story about Elmo Blatch was true. By so doing he signed his own death warrant. In Shawshank, it's not straightforward to differentiate the good guys from the bad guys.

Andy now had only one goal: escape. He had been involved in the planning and preparation of an escape for a long time. Now was the moment of execution. In spite of everything that had happened, Andy still had hope.

TIME TO UPROOT
There is a time to plant and there's a time to pull up what is planted

It's 1966. Andy is getting ready to leave this life, but before he does, he has some final words for his dear friend of nearly 20 years:

"Red. If you ever get out of here, do me a favour."

"Sure, Andy. Anything."

"There's a big hayfield up near Buxton. You know where Buxton is?"

"Well, there's... there's a lot of hayfields up there."

"One in particular. It's got a long rock wall with a big oak tree at the north end. It's like something out of a Robert Frost poem. It's where I asked my wife to marry me. We went there for a picnic and made love under that oak, and I asked and she said yes. Promise me, Red. If you ever get out find that spot. At the base of that wall, you'll find a rock that has no earthly business in a Maine hayfield. Piece of black, volcanic glass. There's something buried under it I want you to have."

"What, Andy? What's buried under there?"

"You'll have to pry it up... to see."

And with that Andy walks off. Red never sees his friend in Shawshank again. Shortly after his disappearance Randall Stephens walks into one of the banks where he has a deposit of funds and closes his account. He does this at several locations amassing a total of $370,000 (circa $20 million in today's money.) A figment of Andy's imagination cleans out the dirty cash that Norton had accumulated over the past 19 years.

The warden has no need of money. He has blown his brains out before the federal agents arrive to arrest him for alleged corruption and murder in Shawshank. Mr Stephens had left a large file of information with the bank to mail to the local newspaper. The evidence was overwhelming. The paper ran large headlines – 'Corruption and murder at Shawshank'.

The cons who saw Hadley being arrested and carted off in handcuffs could hardly believed their eyes. Andy had brought an end to the ruthless regime at Shawshank. For months they spent their meals together jubilantly recalling the various antics of their friend Andy. Red looks on smiling in silent thought.

Sometimes it makes me sad though… Andy being gone. I have to remind myself that some birds aren't meant to be caged. Their feathers are just too bright. And when they fly away, the part of you that knows it was a sin to lock them up DOES rejoice. But still, the place you live in is that much more drab and empty now that they're gone. I guess I just miss my friend.

Red is up for parole. He refuses to play the hypocrite:

"Ellis Boyd Redding, your files say you've served 40 years of a life sentence. Do you feel you've been rehabilitated?"

"Rehabilitated? Well, now let me see. You know, I don't have any idea what that means."

"Well, it means that you're ready to re-join society…"

"I know what you think it means, sonny. To me, it's just a made-up word. A politician's word, so young fellas like yourself can wear a suit and a tie and have a job. What do you really want to know? Am I sorry for what I did?"

"Well, are you?"

"There's not a day goes by I don't feel regret. Not because I'm in here, because you think I should. I look back on the way I was then: a young, stupid kid who committed that terrible crime. I want to talk to him. I want to try to talk some sense to him, tell him the way things are. But I can't. That kid's long gone, and this old man is all that's left. I got to live with that. Rehabilitated? It's just a meaningless word. So you go on and stamp your form, sonny, and stop wasting my time. Because to tell you the truth, I don't care anymore."

His application for parole is stamped 'Approved'. He's a free man. Some days after leaving Shawshank he honours the promise he made to his friend. He gets the bus to Buxton, finds the hayfield, locates the tree and the piece of black, volcanic glass that has no earthly business in a Maine hayfield. Beneath it there's a tin box. In the box there's a wad of cash and a letter that says:

Dear Red. If you're reading this, you've gotten out. And if you've come this far, maybe you're willing to come a little further. You remember the name of the town, don't you? I could use a good man to help me get my project on wheels. I'll keep an eye out for you and the chessboard ready. Remember, Red, hope is a good thing, maybe the best of things, and no good thing ever dies. I will be hoping that this letter finds you and finds you well. Your friend, Andy.

The man who said 'Hope is a dangerous thing; hope can drive a man insane' is having a change of heart. The hope that one person has for another will do that – it will gently make them change the way they think:

I find I am so excited I can barely sit still or hold a thought in my head. I think it's the excitement only a free man can feel; a free man at the start of a long journey whose conclusion is uncertain. I hope I can make it across the border. I hope to see my friend and shake his hand. I hope the Pacific is as blue as it has been in my dreams. I hope.

How did Andy escape? Well let me follow the fine example set by the ladies whose pictures successively adorned the wall of his prison cell: Rita Hayworth, Marilyn Monroe, and finally Raquel Welch. Each one was in her turn the poster lady of their respective decade – 40s, 50s and 60s. Each one kept Andy's secret while he remained in jail. So shall I.

What I will say is that the key that unlocked Shawshank for Andy was **hope**, and he left that key with his fellow inmates.

THE PICTURE'S PARABLE

The story of Andy and the characters in the world that they inhabit is beautifully told in the film *The Shawshank Redemption* (1994). The film was nominated for 7 Oscars and won none (where have we heard that before?!)

Its popularity today is unexcelled. It has occupied the number 1 slot of favourite film of all time in the IMDB charts for several years.

113

A stellar cast was assembled led by Tim Robbins (Andy) and principally starred Morgan Freeman (Red), Bob Gunton (Norton), Clancy Brown (Hadley), and William Sadler (Heywood). Frank Darabont who was in effect showrunner for the movie directed the film.

The original story was the creation of Stephen King whose books I have never read but whose work is clearly monumental. I don't actually know what was in King's mind when he named Andy DuFresne. The French word frêne means ash tree. So Andy is of the ash family, and the ash tree is known for its toughness, lightness, durability, and almost complete resistance to shocks. Well done Mr King if that was your intention.

As ever, I ask myself what is it about this movie that gives it such incredible durability and broad appeal. The story is unmistakably compelling.

Andy is innocent yet suffers grotesque injustice. While in Shawshank there is no sense of self-pity only a commitment to bring hope to others. Far from being self-obsessed, Andy is fully invested in the wellbeing of others.

He makes his plans without ostentation or even hints of what he intends while getting along with all, except The Sisters. Their leader, Bogs, gets his just desserts partly as a consequential benefit from Andy's treatment of the guards. This is another amazing characteristic – Andy makes enemies of none.

The bad guys, posing as 'good guys', do not escape justice. In the end, Norton shoots himself and Hadley is arrested for murder.

It is true that Andy profits from the corruption of Norton whose reign he assuredly terminates, but he justifies making off with Norton's 'auxiliary pension fund' seeing it as compensation for 19 years wrongful incarceration. In that sense he has saved the State of Maine a load of money. Finally, he puts the record straight on corruption and brutality at Shawshank.

But, above all this for me stands the allusion that this is

a parable, maybe the best of them all. It focuses on this principle: **that hope, resting on the truth, will always bring about that which is hoped for.**

If I may, I would now like to give you my version of this parable looking back once again at this amazing film.

There are three things to say about Andy that make him a standout figure. The first of these is that he is a *substitute*. He is an innocent man who is punished for the crimes of another person. He is not a willing substitute – he protests his innocence, nor is he an identifiable substitute, nevertheless that is what he is.

The second thing to say is he is a *befriender* of all. He does not lament the injustice or have a huge pity party; he simply gets on with his life in Shawshank accepting his circumstances while hoping for justice to come through in its own time. While in Shawshank he treats no one as his enemy. He wins over Red and his gang who speak animatedly and lovingly of him at mealtimes long after he's gone. He befriends the guards, including the monster Captain Hadley by providing them with his expertise. He even makes the warden a secret millionaire. Andy is essentially a reconciler and an ambassador of reconciliation – 'get busy living or get busy dying'. He chose life.

The final thing to say about this character is that he is a *victor*. He gives 19 years of his life to Shawshank, but he is undefeated by its regime. On the contrary he is instrumental in its downfall. There would never again be another Norton, another Hadley. The exposure of their combined criminality began a cleansing of Shawshank – a debt owed to Andy.

Who do I know in history who fits this description – substitute, reconciler, and victor? Well one person I can think of is Joseph (the guy in the Bible with the coat of many colours, celebrated in the musical Joseph and the Technicolor dream coat). Joseph was thrown into jail for allegedly abusing the wife of his master, Potiphar. It was she who should have been incarcerated since she lied about this accusation and she was the one who tried to seduce Joseph. They jailed the wrong person.

While in jail, Joseph showed such grace, kindness and organisational skills that the captain of the jail entrusted its operations to him – amazing.

Finally, he was a victor. He got out of jail at the command of Pharaoh and ended up as his second in command in ruling Egypt. Joseph foresaw the famine and prepared for that and so when it came Egypt prospered and all the surrounding nations became dependent on Egypt's granaries. The nation prospered, thanks to Joseph's endurance and resilience.

His brothers who had tried to murder him and set in train the course of Joseph's experiences in Egypt were amazed when they were blessed by him.

He told them *'you intended this (my treatment) for harm, but God intended it for good.'* I can think of only one phrase that captures that attitude – amazing grace.

It's hard to imagine that Andy's treatment was anything other than unjust. But in the end no one else could have brought about such a radical change in Shawshank as he wrought. He could only accomplish it from the inside. He thought he had to become part of the system to learn how to be a crook. In fact, he was joined to that system so that he could make an end of its crookedness.

That is why this film is so powerful. It is a classic Hollywood Parable.

The best of things

There is another famous character in history; his name is Jesus of Nazareth. He can be compared with Andy. The biblical characterisation of Jesus presents him as substitute, befriender, and victor. It talks about his death being substitutionary – 'he who knew no sin (innocent) was made to be sin (punished for our sins) so that through him we might become righteous before God'. It talks about Jesus' ministry being one of reconciliation – making friends of all, treating none as enemies– 'that God was reconciling the world to himself in Christ, not counting people's sins against them'. And it talks about Jesus overcoming death and sin by destroying both in his body on the cross.

When the mob screamed for Jesus to be crucified, the ruler of this world was whipping them up. He thought that by killing Jesus he would win his battle with God. What did he know? He was playing right into God's hands. The death of Jesus was the means God used to put an end to his rebellion and bring about a new regime under his sovereign, merciful, abundantly gracious lordship.

I'm struck by the parallels between the journey of Andy and the ministry of Jesus. That's why I see *The Shawshank Redemption* as a parable, and a magnificent one at that.

I'm not asking you to believe all this but I hope you will, and that hope can make all the difference. I have high hopes always.

ABOUT THE AUTHOR

John Boardman was born in Blackburn
Lancashire, UK. A professional engineer, he
held tenured positions as full Professor at three
universities in the UK. His most recent
appointment was Distinguished Service
Professor at Stevens Institute of Technology in
New Jersey, USA. There he produced two
popular textbooks on systemic thinking. This is
his third theologically oriented book, following
In God's time, and When God sings. He lives
with his wife Alison in Worcestershire, UK.

Printed in Great Britain
by Amazon

41976268R00076